LIBRARY
OKALOOSA - WALTON JUNIOR

Charles Edward Ives, 1874-1954:
A Bibliography of His Music

Charles Edward Ives, 1874-1954:
A Bibliography of His Music
By Dominique-René de Lerma
Indiana University

The Kent State University Press

Copyright © 1970 by Dominique-René de Lerma.
All rights reserved.
ISBN: 0-87338-057-6.
Library of Congress Card Catalogue Number 72-99083.
Manufactured in the United States of America
at the Press of The Oberlin Printing Company.
Designed by Merald E. Wrolstad.
First Edition.

ML
134
I9
D4

LIBRARY
OKALOOSA - WALTON JUNIOR COLLEGE

To Renée Longy,
an ardent missionary of New Music,
with great devotion

32517

Preface

Interest in the music of Charles Ives, which this bibliography
hopes to encourage, has grown during the past decade at a
most substantial rate. This is clearly manifest bibliographically.
Composers of the Americas listed 55 works which had been
published by 1956; the total twelve years later reached
124 titles, not including songs within anthologies. Twenty-two
listings appeared in the December 1963 issue of the *Schwann
Long-Playing Record Catalog*; the total five years later
reached 77, several of which had become "best-sellers."

   Those composers whose music is almost entirely available
from one publisher (e.g., Hindemith, or Cage) appear to have less
need for full bibliographic citation than those whose publisher
varies frequently (as is the case with Bartók or Stravinsky)—
yet a full register of titles is not without merit in any case.
In order for the performer, the scholar, or the librarian to secure
this information, difficulties can be noted which come from
the trade (for commercial, rather than bibliographic, reasons)

among publishers, dealers and agents: it is not always clear
how many editions actually exist, or which firm should be
credited with the publication. This is particularly well exemplified
with Ives, who only made the problems all the greater because
of the exceptional freedom he exercised in using the same
music or title in more than one instance, and the complexities
of relationships which developed, are not always simplified
by the publishers or their title pages.

No work in Ives is possible at this time without repeated
use of the critical biography by Henry and Sidney Cowell
(*Charles Ives and His Music,* New York, Oxford University
Press, 1955, revised in 1969) and of John Kirkpatrick's
monumental bibliography, *A Temporary Mimeographed
Catalogue of the Music Manuscripts and Related Materials of
Charles Edward Ives, 1874–1954, Given by Mrs. Ives to the
Library of the Yale School of Music, September 1955*
[n.p., 1960]. This latter source, originally issued on a limited
basis, is now fortunately being prepared for a new edition.
The systematic notation employed by Kirkpatrick is adopted
in the present bibliography in the manner of an opus number,
but reference to Kirkpatrick's study of the manuscripts
will remain obligatory to the Ives specialist, despite the fact
that Professor Kirkpatrick modestly regards his work as a
"stop-gap." Also employed is the compilation appearing in
*Composers of the Americas; Biographical Data and a Catalog of
Their Works* (v.2, p.90–100) published by the Music Section
of the Pan-American Union in 1956, and reissued in 1962.
This had been based on a similar list which appeared in the
Bulletin of the American Composers Alliance (v.4, no.3, 1955).
These sources were of necessity supplemented by reference
to the holdings of the New York Public Library, of the
Indiana University School of Music Library, and of the Library
of Congress, as well as a wide variety of miscellaneous sources,

such as publishers' announcements and brief references in periodicals.

Several individuals deserve my gratitude and sincere appreciation for their personal assistance. Indiana University's former Associate Music Librarian, James Elrod, was co-compiler of an earlier list of Ives' music (*A Checklist of Music by Charles Edward Ives, 1874-1954*, Bloomington, 1966). Evidence of his help in preparing that register appears in this present volume. Mrs. Sharon Thompson, Administrative Assistant to the Music Librarian (Indiana University), provided extensive help in many ways. Danny R. Wright, a former student member of that staff, is responsible for the original discography draft. A copy of the Publication Index was submitted for verification to the firms involved. Particular appreciation is extended to Miss Helen M. Grady of Associated Music Publishers and to Calvert Bean, Jr., of Theodore Presser, who were exceptionally helpful. Finally I would like to thank Mrs. Jo Zuppan, Editor of the Kent State University Press, for her patience and most valuable help.

D.S.L.

Stockholm
September 12, 1969

Contents

Introduction

The bibliographic citations consist of the following
elements:

1. *Uniform Title.* The work is entered by a uniform
(or, conventional) title, a practice encountered by patrons of
most American music libraries (cf. *Anglo-American cataloging
rules* [*North American text*], Chicago, American Library
Association, 1967, p.145-172, 294-320). This title has been
amplified as needed to specify not only the work in question, but
the particular version involved. The subtitle "selections" is
not employed, and "arr." is qualified in the manner practiced
by the New York Public Library. Cross references are made
from variant titles to the main entry. Titles of works which
may be (temporarily?) lost or thought to be incomplete
are included, but noted accordingly.

2. *Cutter Number.* Each main entry is assigned a unique
Cutter number, based on the librarian's Cutter-Sanborn table.
Reference to these decimal numbers is made in the indexes.

3. *Medium.* If not evident in the title, a note of medium is included.

4. *Poet or Literary Source.* Parenthetically following the medium is mention of the literary stimulus for the work, as this applies to songs, choral works, operas and incidental music. These names and titles have not been verified.[1]

5. *Date.* The year cited is that in which the work was completed. In cases of uncertainty, the most recent date offered by reliable sources (Kirkpatrick, or Cowell) is accepted. A range of several years is included only when this appears justified.

6. *Opus Number.* The catalog number assigned to each work by Kirkpatrick serves as an opus number, even though Ives employed actual opus numbers for a few works.

7. *Alternate Title.* Subtitles and other variants are noted, including translations as justified by their use in publications.

8. *Duration.* Some concept of the length of the work is registered here when indicated by the composer, the publisher, or a previous cataloger (e.g., the Library of Congress). In actual performance, these durations will quite naturally be subject to variation.

9. *Notes.* Mention is made here of any pertinent bibliographic factor not suitable for inclusion elsewhere.

---

[1] Verification is that process whereby a cataloger establishes a particular spelling, or name form, and date as the consistent and official version to be used by the library in question. This bibliography seeks to verify uniform titles of works by Ives, as well as name forms of those engaged in recorded performances of his works. These decisions are based on the standard verification sources for music and musicians in that priority employed by the major American music libraries. The names of poets and librettists have not been verified; few music libraries have need of verified name forms for them. When they are employed, the library will possibly have its own sources for verification.

10. *Contents.* Full contents are registered, including titles
or tempo indications of the movements, as available.

11. *Publications.* The register of imprints includes publisher,
year of issue, series note, plate number, notes relative to the
specific edition, and the order number of Library of Congress
cards. Those anthologies wherein the work might be found
are merely cited. Publication information in these instances is
registered under the appropriate heading (e.g., *Songs and
harmonizations, Sacred songs*). In the case of those song
anthologies without distinctive publishers' titles (e.g., *114 songs*)
the user will note the location of the main entry within the
anthology, publication information on which is cited under
the entry for the anthology (note, however, that all anthologies
have not been published).

12. *Recordings.* Reference within the bibliography is to
label numbers. Details on performance can be secured from
the Phonorecord Index.

13. *Cross References.* Following "x:" are those titles for
which no main entry has been made, from which the user is
referred to the present title. This will apply to subtitles, alternate
titles, and to those contents with distinctive (not tempo) titles.
When cross references are made from the first lines of a text,
an ellipsis follows.

14. *"See Also" References.* Those titles given after "sa:"
refer to other main entries within the bibliography which
are related to the present main entry, as in the case of
two works bearing similar titles.

The indexes refer from various heading to specific works
by use of the Cutter number, if not also the title.

1. *Publication Index.* Those publishers who have issued the
work of Ives are listed alphabetically by last (or principal)

name, with addresses and agent relationships. Cross references within this alphabet are provided as needed.

2. *Medium Index.* References are made under those subject headings for medium employed by the Library of Congress, but this index is designed to serve more the needs of the performer than the librarian. Some modifications have accordingly been employed.

3. *Chronological Index.* The order in which the works were created is given alphabetically under the year of completion.

4. *Index of Arrangers, Poets and Librettists.* Reference to specific works is made in this index for those persons whose texts were set by Ives. The entries include dates and names as they were available, but these have not been verified for use by librarians.

5. *Phonorecord Index.* This index includes all commercially available phonodiscs, both current and out of print. The listing is alphabetic-numerical by the name of the label, with arrangement priority given to those labels without alphabetic prefixes. Stereophonic (–compatible) labels and references are cited with an "st" suffix. This is not properly part of the label number or the Library of Congress card number. Rather than repeat identical notes on performers and contents for both monaural and stereophonic releases under the same basic label, cross references are employed. No effort has been undertaken to relate possibly identical pressings issued under totally different labels, even though such reference may seem justified at times. The initial line of each entry will include a collation note, giving the total number of sides, size of the recording, and speed (33 1/3rpm will be indicated as "33rpm") when these factors are known. Following this is the order number for Library of Congress cards, with "st" added to those numbers when appropriate. Distinctive titles for the album when employed are given on the second line.

Works included in the recording by Ives are cited by the corresponding Cutter number and a brief title. The list of performers which follows does not include verified name forms (these may be secured from the Performer Index). Those persons engaged in the performance of works by other composers are not cited. A "with" note concludes the entry, listing brief titles of works by composers other than Ives. When this list is particularly long, the titles have been omitted.

6. *Performer index.* This index includes the verified name forms for persons and ensembles engaged in the aforementioned recordings, to which reference is made by label numbers to the Phonorecord index. Verification of names is based on the official catalog of the Indiana University School of Music Library, which includes Library of Congress proof slips interfiled with the authority file. Names not registered in this source are accepted as given on the recording.

Research for information included in this bibliography was terminated on July 1, 1969.

Bibliography

A14 Abide with me.
  Medium voice & piano (Rev. Henry Francis Lyte).
  1890 (?); 6B12.
  Published:
      (1) 6AK no. 1.
      (2) Sacred songs.
  Recorded:
      (1) Overtone LP-7.
  sa:
      (1) Hymn anthem on Abide with me.
      (2) Prelude on Abide with me.

Accept you these emblems . . .
  see: Flag song.

Across the hill of late . . .
  see: Spring song.

8

A19 Adagio, organ, 3D7, F major.
   1892 (?).
   Notes: Incomplete; unfinished or lost.—Title from
      Kirkpatrick.

Adagio: The Indians.
   see: Set, orchestra, no. 5, 1C37.

Adagio sostenuto, orchestra.
   see: Set, orchestra, no. 3, 1C35.

A23 Adeste fideles in an organ prelude.
   1897; 3D19.
   Published:
         (1) Music Press (Mercury), 1949 (Music Press
            organ series MP-601), published with his
            Variations on America; 50-28932rev2/M.
   Recorded:
         (1) Nonesuch H-71200.
   sa:
         (1) Slow march on Adeste fideles, band.
         (2) Variations on America, organ.

Adieu, adieu! . . .
   see: A farewell to land.

A25 Aeschylus and Sophocles.
   Voice & piano (Walter Savage Landor).
   1922; 6AD6.
   Published:
         (1) 6AD no. 6.
   x:
         (1) We also have our pest . . .

After trying hard to think . . .
   see: Vote for names.

A26 Afterglow.
Voice & piano (James Fenimore Cooper, Jr.).
1919; 6B60c.
Published:
(1) 6AA no. 39.
(2) 6AC no. 10.
(3) 6Ae no. 1.
Recorded:
(1) Folkways FM-3344/5.
x:
(1) At the quiet close of day . . .

A27 Age of gold.
TTBB.
1896 (?); 5D8.
Notes: Lost.

Ah! s'il est dans votre village . . .
see: Chanson de Florian.

Alas! for them their day is o'er . . .
see: The Indians.

A41 The all-enduring, chorus & orchestra.
(Judge Lyman D. Brewster [?]).
1896 (?); 5B1.
Notes: Lost.
x:
(1) Man passes down the way of years . . .

A41b The all-enduring, voice & piano.
(Judge Lyman D. Brewster [?]).
1896 (?); 6B23.
Published:
(1) 6Ab no. 1.
x:
(1) Man passes down the way of years . . .

A42 All-forgiving.
   Vocal quartet (Ray Palmer, trans., from *Salve mundi salutare*, v.2).
   1898 (?); 5C31.
   sa:
      (1) Life of the world.

A43 All love that has not friendship . . .
   Voice & piano.
   1892; 6B15.

A44 All the way around and back.
   Instrumental ensemble.
   1906 (?); 2B12
   Published:
      (1) Peer, 196–.
   sa:
      (1) Set of cartoons or take-offs.

   Allegretto sombreoso.
   see: When the moon is on the wave.

A45 Allegro, violin & piano.
   1907; not in Kirkpatrick.
   Notes: Cited in *Composers of the Americas* as a fragment.

A46 Allegro, voice & piano.
   (Charles E. Ives).
   1900 (?); 6B35d.
   Published:
      (1) 6AA no. 95.
      (2) 6AK no. 6.
   x:
      (1) By morning's brightest beams . . .

   Allegro moderato, orchestra
   see: The gong on the hook and ladder.

A48 Alone upon the housetops . . .
Voice & piano (Rudyard Kipling, from *The love song of Har Dyal*).
1898 (?); 6B29b.
Published:
(1) 6Aa no. 3.
(2) 6Ab no. 4.
x:
(1) The love song of Har Dyal.
(2) Poems of Kipling.

America.
see: Variations on America, organ.

A49 The American woods overture.
Orchestra.
1899 (?); 1C2.
Notes: Lost.

A52 Amphion.
Voice & piano (Alfred Lord Tennyson).
1896; 6B24a.
Published:
(1) 6AA no. 106.
(2) 6AA bis.
(3) 6AF no. 5 (under title: From Amphion).
x:
(1) From Amphion.
(2) The mountain stirred its bushy crown . . .

And in September . . .
see: September.

And so he came . . .
see: Lincoln, the great commoner.

Andante cantabile: The last reader.
see: Set, orchestra, no. 4, 1C36.

A61 Ann Street.
Voice & piano (Maurice Morris).
1921 (?); 6B67.
Published:
(1) 6AA no. 25
(2) 6AC no. 2.
Recorded:
(1) Cambridge 804; CRS-1804st.
(2) Folkways FM-3344/5.
(3) Nonesuch H-71209st.
(4) NMQR-1412.
(5) Overtone LP-7.
x:
(1) Quant name . . .
sa:
(1) Set, orchestra, no. 6, 1C38.

A62 Anthem, chorus, 5C32.
1898; 5C32.
Notes: Lost.

Anthem-processional.
see: Psalm 135.

A63 The anti-abolitionist riots.
Piano.
1908 (?); 3B17/9.
Notes: No. 9 of Studies, piano.
Published:
(1) Mercury (Presser), 1949; pl. no. 189.
Recorded:
(1) Folkways FM-3348.
x: Studies, piano.

Arguments.
see: Quartet, strings, no. 2.

Arnold overture.
see: Matthew Arnold overture.

As pants the hart . . .
see: Psalm 42.

A86 At parting.
Voice & piano (Frederic Peterson).
1889; 6B10c.
Published:
(1) 6AC no. 34.
Recorded:
(1) Society of Participating Artists SPA-9.
x:
(1) The sweetest flow'r . . .

A87 At sea.
Voice & piano (Robert Underwood Johnson).
1921; 6B63a.
Published:
(1) 6AA no. 4.
(2) 6AC no. 3.
(3) 6AB bis.
(4) 6AA bis.
Recorded:
(1) Society of Participating Artists SPA-9.
x:
(1) Some things are undivined . . .
sa:
(1) Set, orchestra, no. 3, 1C35.

At the quiet close of day . . .
see: Afterglow.

A88 At the river.
   Voice & piano (Robert Lowry).
   1916; 6B54.
   Published:
      (1) 6AA no. 45.
      (2) 6AC no. 13.
   Recorded:
      (1) Concert Hall CHC-7.
      (2) Nonesuch H-71209.
      (3) Overtone LP-7.
      (4) Society of Participating Artists SPA-9.
   x:
      (1) Shall we gather at the river . . .

A92 August.
   Voice & piano (Folgore da San Geminiano; Dante Gabriel
      Rossetti, trans.)
   1920; 6B61a.
   Published:
      (1) 6AA no. 35.
      (2) 6AG no. 7.
   x:
      (1) For August be your dwelling . . .

   Autumn.
   see: Sonata, violin & piano, no. 2.

A93 Autumn, 6B40e.
   Voice & piano.
   1902.
   Notes: Lost.—Title from Kirkpatrick.

A94 Autumn, 6B45.
   Voice & piano (Harmony T. Ives).
   1908.

Published:

    (1) 6AA no. 60.

    (2) 6AJ no. 5.

Recorded:

    (1) Overtone LP-7.

x:

    (1) Earth rests! . . .

A95 Autumn landscape from Pine Mountain.
    Orchestra.
    1904; 1C20.
    Notes: Lost.

  Battell chimes.
    see: The bells of Yale.

B36 Be thou, O God, exalted high . . .
    Chorus (Psalm 108/5).
    1892 (?); 5C16.
    Notes: Lost.
    x:

        (1) Psalm 108, v5.

  Be ye in love . . .
    see: In April tide.

  Beautiful river.
    see: Piece on Beautiful river, orchestra.

B38 Because of you.
    Voice & piano.
    1898; 6B30.
    x:

        (1) What have you done for me . . .

B44 The bells of Yale.
Baritone, TTBB & piano (Huntington Mason).
1897 (?); 5D11.
Alternate title: Battell chimes.
Published:
> (1) New Haven, Th. G. Shepard. 1903 (Yale melodies, p.88–92).

x:
> (1) Battell chimes.
> (2) Ring out, sweet chime . . .

B46 Benedictus, 5C9, E major.
Chorus (St. Luke).
1888–1890 (?).
x:
> (1) Blessed be the Lord God of Israel . . .

B47 Benedictus, 5C13, G major.
Chorus (St. Luke).
1891 (?).
Notes: Lost.
x:
> (1) Blessed be the Lord God of Israel . . .

B48 Berceuse.
Voice & piano (Charles E. Ives).
1900 (?); 6B41d.
Published:
> (1) 6AA no. 93.
> (2) 6AA bis.
> (3) 6AK no. 7.

Recorded:
> Overtone LP-7.

x:
O'er the mountain . . .

Between the dark and daylight . . .
    see: The children's hour.

A big October morning . . .
    see: Walking.

Bland air and leagues . . .
    see: A perfect day.

Die blauen Frühlingsaugen . . .
    see: Frühlingslied.

Blaw, skirlin', win' . . .
    see: A Scotch lullaby.

Blessed be the Lord God of Israel . . .
    see: Beneductus, 5C9, E major.
        Benedictus, 5C13, G major.

Booth led boldly . . .
    see: General William Booth's entrance into heaven.

Boston Common.
    see: Three places in New England.

B82 Bread of the world.
    Chorus (Reginald Heber).
    1891 or 1982 (?); 5C14.
    Notes: Incomplete; unfinished or lost (?).

Breathe from the gentle South . . .
    see: The waiting soul.

Browning overture.
    see: Robert Browning overture.

B96 Burlesque storm.
 2 pianos.
 1896; 3C1.
 Notes: Lost or incomplete.—Title from Kirkpatrick.

By morning's brightest beams . . .
 see: Allegro, voice & piano.

Byron's When the moon is on the wave.
 see: When the moon is on the wave.

C13 The cage.
 Voice & piano (Charles E. Ives).
 1906; 6B42.
 Published:
  (1) 6AA no. 64.
  (2) 6AH no. 8.
  (3) also reprinted as a single-leaf insert in
   Set for theatre or chamber orchestra.
 Recorded:
  (1) Cambridge 804; CRS-1804st.
  (2) Concert Hall CHC-7.
  (3) Folkways FM-3344/5.
  (4) Nonesuch H-71209st.
 x:
  (1) A leopard went around his cage.
 sa:
  (1) Set for theatre or chamber orchestra.

C14 Calcium light night (1898–1907).
 2 pianos, winds & percussion.
 1907 (?); 1C31/v.
 Duration: 2'30".
 Notes: No. 5 of Set, orchestra, no. 1, 1C31—Publication

of this title in New Music, v.24 [i.e., v26], no.4,
is actually of The gong on the hook and ladder.
Published:

    (1) Presser; ed. by Henry Cowell, rental.

x:

    (1) Set, orchestra, no. 1, 1C31.

sa:

    (1) The gong on the hook and ladder.

C15 Calcium light night (1898–1907); arr., chamber orchestra.
Notes: Simplification of C14, arranged by Henry Cowell
in 1936 on request of Ives. A copy is held by the
New York Public Library.

The call of the mountains.
see: Quartet, strings, no. 2.

C18 The camp meeting.
Medium voice & piano (Charles E. Ives, after
Charlotte Elliott).
1912; 6B48b.
Published:

    (1) 6AA no. 47.
    (2) 6AK no. 10.
    (3) Sacred songs.

sa:

    (1) Symphony, no. 3.

C22 Canon: Not only in my lady's eyes.
Voice & piano.
1893; 6B16.

x:

    (1) Not only in my lady's eyes . . .

C23 Canon: Oh, the days are gone.
    Voice & piano (Thomas Moore).
    1894; 6B20c.
    Published:
        (1) 6AA no. 111.
        (2) 6AD no. 8.
    Recorded:
        (1) Duke.
        (2) Folkways FM-3344/5.
    x:
        (1) Oh, the days are gone . . .

Canticle phrases.
    see: Experimental canticle phrases.

C24 Canzonetta, organ, 3D8, F major.
    1893 (?).
    Notes: Title from Kirkpatrick.

Cartoons or take-offs.
    see: Set of cartoons or take-offs.

C38 The celestial country. English.
    Cantata (Henry Alford, thought by Ives to be after
        St. Bernard of Cluny).
    1898-1899; 5A1.
    Contents: (1) Prelude, trio, chorus, prelude (Far o'er
        yon horizon).—(2) Aria, baritone (Naught that
        country needeth).—(3) Quartet, accompanied interlude
        (Seek the things before us).—(4) Intermezzo for string
        quartet, interlude.—(5) Octet a cappella (Glories).—
        (6) Aria, tenor (Forward, flock of Jesus).—(7) Chorale
        and finale (To the eternal Father).

Published:

> (1) Ives, n.d. ?; contains nos. 1 & 7 only.
> (2) Peer, 196-.

sa:

> Forward into light.

C39 The celestial country. Naught that country needeth.
Baritone & piano (Henry Alford).
Published:

> (1) 6AA no. 98.
> (2) 6AA bis.
> (3) 6AH no. 5.
> (4) Sacred songs.

x:

> (1) Naught that country needeth . . .

C395 The celestial railroad.
Piano.
1916; 3B19.

C41 Central Park in the dark.
Orchestra.
1906; 1C27.
Alternate title: 2d movement of Two contemplations.
Published:

> (1) Bomart, 1949, in Outdoor scenes; publication
> disclaimed by Associated Music Publishers,
> who has this title on rental only.

Recorded:

> (1) Columbia ML-6243.
> (2) Composers Recordings Inc. CRI-163.
> (3) Polymusic PRLP-1001, under title Pieces for
> orchestra.

x:

    (1) Contemplations.

    (2) Outdoor scenes.

    (3) Pieces for orchestra.

C45 Chanson de Florian.
Medium voice & piano (J.P. Claris, Chevalier de Florian).
1901 (?); 6B27b.
Published:

    (1) 6AA no. 78.

    (2) Mercury (Presser), 1950.

x:

    (1) Ah! s'il est dans votre village . . .

C46 Chant, op. 2, no. 2.
Chorus (textless).
1887 (?); 5C2.

C47 Charlie Rutlage.
Voice & piano (cowboy ballad).
1914 or 1915 (?); 6B51a.
Published:

    (1) 6AA no. 10.

    (2) 6AA bis.

    (3) 6AB no. 2.

    (4) Arrow (Associated Music Publishers), 1939.

Recorded:

    (1) Columbia CLPS-1008.

    (2) Duke.

    (3) Educo 4006.

    (4) Folkways FM-3344/5.

    (5) NMQR-1412.

    (6) Nonesuch H-71209st.

C48 Charlie Rutlage, orchestra.
    1922 (?); 1C40.
    Notes: Orchestration of C47 only projected.

Children's day.
    see: Symphony, no. 3.

Children's day at the camp meeting.
    see: Sonata, violin & piano, no. 4.

C53 Children's day parade.
    Organ.
    1901 (?); 3D20
    Notes: Lost.
    x:
        (1) Postlude: Children's day parade.

C54 The children's hour.
    Voice & piano (Henry Wadsworth Longfellow)
    1901 (?); 6B38.
    Published:
        (1) 6AA no. 74.
        (2) 6AA bis.
        (3) 6AC no. 28.
    Recorded:
        (1) Concert Hall CHC-7.
        (2) Folkways FM-3344/5.
        (3) Overtone LP-7.
    x:
        (1) Between dark and daylight . . .

C55 Chorale for strings in quarter-tones.
    1913–1914 (?); 2B19.
    Notes: Lost.

C56 Chorale for strings in quarter-tones, 2 pianos.
1913–1914 (?); 2B19.
Notes: Lost (?).

C57 Christ, our passover . . .
Chorus (St. Paul).
1890 or 1891 (?); 5C5.
Alternate title: Easter anthem (Kirkpatrick).
Notes: Incomplete; unfinished or lost (?).
x:
(1) Easter anthem.

Christian and pagan.
see: Slants, or Christian and pagan.

C58 A Christmas carol.
Voice & piano (Charles E. Ives, harmonizer).
1898 (?); 6B27d.
Published:
(1) 6AA no. 100.
(2) 6AA bis.
(3) 6AD no. 15.
(4) Songs and harmonizations.
Recorded:
(1) Folkways FM-3344/5.
(2) Society for the Preservation of the American
Musical Heritage MTA-116.
(3) Society of Participating Artists SPA-9.
(4) Nonesuch H-71209st.
x:
(1) Little star of Bethlehem . . .

C59 Chromâtimelôdtune.
Piano.
1909 or 1919 (?); 2B20.

Notes: No. 27 of Studies, piano.
Recorded:
    (1) Nonesuch H-71222st; in arrangement for brasses.
x:
    (1) Studies, piano.

C61 Chromâtimelôdtune; arr., chamber orchestra.
    Not in Kirkpatrick.
    Duration: 6′.
    Notes: Reconstructed and completed by Gunther Schuller
    in 1962.
    Published:
        (1) New York, MJQ, 1967 (MPQ, 16); copyright
        1963, score on sale, parts rental; 67-125466/M
        (score).

C62 Circus band, chorus & orchestra.
    SSATTBB & orchestra.
    1894; not in Kirkpatrick.
    Published:
        (1) Peer, [n.d. ?].
    Recorded:
        (1) Columbia ML-6821.

C63 Circus band, orchestra.
    1894 (?); 1C8.
    x:
        (1) March: The circus band.

C64 Circus band, piano.
    1894 (?); 3B12.

C65 Circus band, voice & piano.
    (Charles E. Ives).
    1894; 6B20.

Published:
 (1) 6AA no. 56.
 (2) 6AA bis.
 (3) 6AF no. 3.
Recorded:
 (1) Concert Hall CHC-7.
x:
 (1) All summer long . . .

C66 Circus band, voice & piano; voice & orchestra.
 (Charles E. Ives).
 1894 (?); 6B20.
 Notes: Arranged by Ives and George F. Roberts.

C67 Circus band, voice & piano; arr., orchestra.
 (Charles E. Ives).
 Not in Kirkpatrick.
 Duration: 3'36".
 Notes: Arranged by Harold Farberman.
 Recorded:
  (1) Vanguard VCS-10013st.

C69 The collection.
 Medium voice & piano (George Kingsley).
 1920; 6B60e.
 Published:
  (1) 6AA no. 38.
  (2) 6AK no. 12
  (3) Secred songs.
 x:
  (1) Now help us, Lord . . .

Come, ye thankful people . . .
 see: Harvest home chorale.

Come away to the manger . . .
 see: Edie's carol.

Come join my humble ditty . . .
    see: A son of a gambolier.

Communion.
    see: Symphony, no. 3.

C73 Communion service.
    SATB.
    1890–1891; 5C12.
    Notes: Unfinished.—Sketches include settings of Kyrie,
       Gloria and Gratias tibi, Sanctus, Credo, Benedictus,
       Agnus Dei, and Sursum corda.

Concord sonata.
    see: Sonata, piano, no. 2.

Contemplations.
    see: The unanswered question.
       Central Park in the dark.

Contented river.
    see: The Housatonic at Stockbridge.

A cosmic landscape.
    see: The unanswered question.

C85 Country band march.
    Band.
    1902; 1C14.

C86 Country celestial.
    Voice & piano (John Mason Neale, trans.)
    1890 or 1891 (?); 6B12a.
    x:
         (1) For thee, O dear, dear country . . .

C88 Cradle song.
  Voice & piano (A. L. Ives).
  1919; 6B60a.
  Published:
      (1) 6AA no. 33.
      (2) 6AA bis.
      (3) 6AD no. 4.
  Recorded:
      (1) Concert Hall CHC-7.
  x:
      (1) Hush thee, dear child . . .

C95 Crossing the bar.
  Chorus (Alfred Lord Tennyson).
  1891 (?); 5C7.
  x:
      (1) Sunset and evening star . . .

  Crouch'd on the pavement . . .
  see: West London.

D17 Danbury fair skit.
  Orchestra.
  1902; 1C13.
  Notes: Lost.
  x:
      (1) Skit for Danbury fair.

D28 December.
  Unison men's voices & 11 wind instruments (Folgore da
      San Geminiano; Dante Gabriel Rossetti, trans.)
  1912–1913; 5B6.
  Duration: 1'30".
  Published: Peer, 1963 (580-12 [score], 580a-1 [parts],
      812-2 [chorus part]); 63-51681/M.

Recorded:
>   (1) Columbia ML-6321.

x:
>   (1) Last, for December . . .

D29 December, voice & piano.
(Folgore da San Geminiano; Dante Gabriel Rossetti, trans.)
1920 (?); 6B49b.
Published:
>   (1) 6AA no. 37.
>   (2) 6AC no. 18.

x:
>   (1) Last, for December . . .

Decoration Day.
see: Holidays.

D36 Delta Kappa Epsilon.
Song with chorus.
1896 or 1897 (?); 4A5.

Delta Kappa Epsilon show, 4A4, Hell's bells.
see: Hell's bells.

D37 Delta Kappa Epsilon sketch, 4A3.
1896; 4A3.
Notes: Lost.

D38 Delta Kappa Epsilon spring show.
1896 (?); 4A2.
Notes: Lost.

D61 Disclosure.
Medium voice & piano (Charles E. Ives).
1921 (?); 6B67b.

Published:
  (1) 6AA no. 7.
  (2) 6AA bis.
  (3) 6AG no. 12.
  (4) Sacred songs.
Recorded:
  (1) Overtone LP-7.
x:
  (1) Thoughts which deeply rest . . .

Discussions.
  see: Quartet, strings, no. 2.

Do'st remember child . . .
  see: Kären.

D68 Don't you see . . .
  Voice & piano.
  1909 (?); 6B45c.
  Notes: Unfinished.

D74 Down east.
  Voice & piano (Charles E. Ives).
  1919; 6B60b.
  Published:
    (1) 6AA no. 55.
    (2) 6AK no. 11.
    (3) Sacred songs.
  x:
    (1) Songs! Visions of my homeland . . .

D75 Down east overture.
  1897 or 1898 (?); 1C10.
  Notes: Lost.

Down the river comes a noise . . .
    see: The new river.

Down with politicians.
    see: An election.

D77 Dream sweetly.
    Voice & piano.
    1897 (?); 6B27c.
    Notes: Title from Kirkpatrick.

D78 Dreams.
    Voice & piano (trans. from Baroness Porteous).
    1897; 6B25b.
    Published:
        (1) 6AA no. 85.
        (2) 6AJ no. 2.
    x:
        (1) When twilight comes . . .

D79 Drum corps or scuffle.
    Piano, 4 hands.
    ca. 1902; 3C2.

Du alte Mutter . . .
    see: The old mother, 6B36b.

D81 Du bist wie eine Blume.
    Voice & piano (Heinrich Heine).
    1897 (?); 6B25c.

Duty.
    see: Slants, Christian and pagan.

The earth is the Lord's . . .
    see: Psalm 24.

Earth rests!...
> see: Autumn, 6B45.

Easter anthem.
> see: Christ, our passover . . .

E13 Easter carol.
> Vocal quartet, chorus & organ.
> 1892; 5C19.
> Published:
>> (1) Ives, ca. 1902; lithographed.
> x:
>> (1) Wake! Wake, earth . . .

E23 Edie's carol.
> Voice & piano (Edith Osborne Ives Tyler).
> 1925; 6B76.
> Published:
>> (1) Ives, 1925; lithographed.

E38 An election.
> Chorus & orchestra (Charles E. Ives).
> 1920; 5B12.
> Alternate title: November 2, 1920.—Down with politicians.
> x:
>> (1) November 2, 1920.
>> (2) It strikes me that . . .
>> (3) Down with politicians.

E39 An election, voice & piano.
> Medium voice & piano (Charles E. Ives).
> 1921; 6B65b.
> Published:
>> (1) 6AA no. 22.
>> (2) 6AD no. 12.
>> (3) Mercury, 1950.

Recorded:
>   (1) Cambridge 804; CRS-1804st.
>   (2) Folkways FM-3344/5.

x:
>   (1) It strikes me that . . .

E41 Elégie.
>   Voice & piano (Louis Gallet).
>   1901 (?); 6B38b.
>   Published:
>   >   (1) 6AA no. 77.
>   >   (2) 6AA bis.
>   >   (3) 6AJ no. 3.
>   x:
>   >   (1) O doux printemps . . .

An elegy to our forefathers.
>   see: Orchestral set, no. 2.

E53 Emerson overture.
>   1907; 1B5/1.
>   Notes: No. 1 (?) of Men of literature overtures.
>   x:
>   >   (1) Men of literature overtures.

E56 The ending year.
>   Voice & piano.
>   1902; 6B40d.
>   x:
>   >   (1) Frail autumn lights . . .

E93 Evening.
>   Voice & piano (John Milton).
>   1921; 6B69a.

Published:

    (1) 6AA no. 2.

    (2) 6AA bis.

    (3) 6AB no. 1.

    (4) Arrow (Associated Music Publishers), 1939;
        pl. no. B2.

Recorded:

    (1) Folkways FM-3344/5.

    (2) NMQR-1412.

    (3) Nonesuch H-71209st.

    (4) Overtone LP-7.

x:

    (1) Now came still evening . . .

E94 Evidence.

Voice & piano (Charles E. Ives).

1910; 6B46a.

Published:

    (1) 6AA no. 58.

    (2) 6AJ no. 6.

x:

    (1) There comes o'er the valley . . .

E96 Experimental canticle phrases.

Chorus.

1891 or 1892 (?); 5C6.

Notes: Contains 9 items, the first three of which are
based on words of the Venite, followed by a textless
movement, a movement entitled Magnificat, three textless
movements and a movement entitled Benedictus.

x:

    (1) Canticle phrases.

Eyes so dark . . .
  see: Weil' auf mir.

F21 Fantasia on Jerusalem the golden, band.
　　1888 or 1891; 1D5.
　　Notes: Lost.
　　x:
　　　　(1) Jerusalem the golden.

F22 Far from my heaven'ly home.
　　Voice & piano (Rev. Henry Francis Lyte).
　　1890; 6B11.
　　Published:
　　　　(1) Songs and harmonizations.

F23 Far in the wood.
　　Voice & piano.
　　1894 (?); 6B20b.

F24 A farewell to land.
　　Voice & piano (Lord Byron).
　　1909; 6B46.
　　Published:
　　　　(1) 6AD no. 2.
　　Recorded:
　　　　(1) Cambridge 804; CRS-1804st.
　　　　(2) Folkways FM-3344/5.
　　　　(3) Nonesuch H-71204st.
　　x:
　　　　(1) Adieu, adieu! . . .

F29 La fède.
　　Voice & piano (Ludovico Ariosto).
　　1920; 6B61.
　　Published:
　　　　(1) 6AA no. 34.
　　　　(2) 6AA bis.
　　　　(3) 6AD no. 5.

Feldeinsamkeit.
see: In summer fields.

Fifteen years ago today . . .
see: He is there! May 30, 1917.

Fill, fill, fill . . .
see: Pass the can along.

Fireman's parade on Main Street.
see: The gong on the hook and ladder.

First hymn.
see: Hymn, 5C1.

F57 Flag song.
Voice & piano (Henry Strong Durand).
1898; 6B31.
Published:
(1) Peer, 1968; 68-129374/M.
x:
(1) Accept you these emblems . . .

The fool hath said in his heart . . .
see: Psalm 14.

For long I wander'd happily . . .
see: The world's highway.

For August be your dwelling . . .
see: August.

For God is glorified in man . . .
see: Paracelsus.

For the grandeur of thy nature . . .
see: His exaltation.

For thee, o dear, dear country . . .
see: Country celestial.

F69 For you and me.
    TTBB.
    ca. 1896; 5D7.
    Published:
        (1) George Molineux, 1896 (Molineux' Collection
        of part songs and choruses for male voices, no. 966).

Forefather's Day.
    see: Holidays.

The Fourth of July.
    see: Holidays.

F74 Forward into light.
    Soprano or tenor & piano (Henry Alford?).
    ca. 1899; 6AA99.
    Notes: Taken from Forward, flock of Jesus, in The
        celestial country, with new text possibly by Ives.
    Published:
        (1) 6AA no. 99.
        (2) 6AA bis.
        (3) 6AF no. 7.
        (4) Sacred songs.
    x:
        (1) The celestial country.

Frail autumn lights . . .
    see: The ending year.

From Amphion.
    see: Amphion.

From Hanover Square.
    see: Orchestral set, no. 2.

From the incantation.
    see: The incantation.

38

From "Lincoln, the great commoner."
see: Lincoln, the great commoner.

F93 From the steeples.
Orchestra; bells (chimes) or 2 pianos, trumpet & trombone.
1901; 1C12.
Alternate title: From the steeples and the mountains.
Published:
(1) Peer, 1965; pl. no. 980-8; 66-54002/M.
Recorded:
(1) Nonesuch H-71222st.
x:
(1) From the steeples and the mountains.

From the steeples and the mountains.
see: From the steeples.

From the swimmers.
see: The swimmers.

F94 Frühlingslied.
Voice & piano (Heinrich Heine).
1896; 6B25.
x:
(1) Die blauen Frühlingsaugen . . .

Fugue, orchestra, C minor.
see: Symphony, no. 4.

F95 Fugue, organ, 3D14, C minor.
1897 (?).

F96 Fugue, organ, 3D15, E flat major.
1897.

F97 Fugue, string quartet, 2B2, B flat major.
1895 (?).
Notes: Mostly lost.

F98 Fugue, string quartet, 2B3, D major.
1895 (?).
Notes: Mostly lost.

F99 Fugue, string quartet, 2B4.
1895 (?); 2B4.
Alternate title: On shining shore.—Fugue in four keys.
Notes: Unfinished (?).
x:
(1) Fugue in four keys.
(2) On shining shore.

Fugue, string quartet, 2B5.
see: Greek fugue in four keys, string quartet.

Fugue in four keys.
see: Fugue, string quartet, 2B4.
Greek fugue in four keys, string quartet.

Full fathom five thy father lies . . .
see: A sea dirge.

G32 The General Slocum, July 1904.
Orchestra.
1904; 1B4.
Notes: Unfinished (?).

G33 General William Booth's entrance into heaven.
Voice & piano (N. Vachel Lindsay).
1914; 6B50.
Published:
(1) New Music, 1935, v.9, no.1.
(2) 6AD no. 1.
Recorded:
(1) NMQR-1112.
(2) Desto D-411/412.

      (3) Cambridge 804; CRS-1804st.
      (4) Folkways FM-3344/5.
      (5) Nonesuch H-71209st.
      (6) Overtone LP-7.

   x:

      (1) Booth led boldly . . .

G34 General William Booth's entrance into heaven,
   mixed voices & band.
      Chorus or solo voice & band (N. Vachel Lindsay).
      1914; 5B9.
      x:

      (1) Booth led boldly . . .

G35 General William Booth's entrance into heaven,
   mixed voices & orchestra.
      Chorus or solo voice & orchestra (N. Vachel Lindsay).
      Not in Kirkpatrick.
      Duration: 4 minutes.
      Published:
      (1) Presser, n.d. (?).

G36 General William Booth's entrance into heaven;
   arr., chamber orchestra.
      1934; cited in Kirkpatrick, p. 125.
      Notes: Arranged by John J. Becker; may be identical to **G34**.
      Published:
      (1) Presser. n.d. (?); rental.
      Recorded:
      (1) Columbia ML-6321.

   Giants vs. Cubs.
      see: Set of cartoons or take-offs.

G56 Gloria in excelsis.
   Chorus.
   1890 or 1891 (?); 5C4.
   Notes: Incomplete; unfinished or lost (?).
   x:
      (1) Glory be to God on high . . .

   Glory be to God on high . . .
      see: Gloria in excelsis.

   Go, my songs! . . .
      see: Old home day.

   God be merciful unto us . . .
      see: Psalm 67.

G57 God bless and keep thee.
   Voice & piano (anonymous).
   1897 (?); 6B25a.
   Published:
      (1) Songs and harmonizations.
   x:
      (1) I know not if thee love . . .

G58 God of my life.
   Chorus & organ (Charlotte Elliott).
   1892 (?); 5C18.
   Notes: Organ part missing.

G63 The gong on the hook and ladder.
   Chamber orchestra.
   1911 (?); 1C30.
   Alternate title: Firemen's parade on Main Street.—
      Space and duration (title from sketches).

Published:

> (1) New Music, 1953, v.24 [i.e., v.26], no. 4; published
> under title Calcium light night; M53-1906rev2.
> (2) Peer, 1960; published with score and parts
> under title Allegro moderato; 63-29837/M.

x:

> (1) Allegro moderato, orchestra.
> (2) Firemen's parade on Main Street.
> (3) Space and duration.

sa:

> (1) Calcium light night (1898-1907).

Good night, my care and my sorrow . . .
see: The sea of sleep.

G72 Grace.
Voice & piano.
ca. 1899; 6B33.
x:

> (1) We in this world today . . .

G76 Grantchester.
Voice & piano (Rupert Brooke).
1920; 6B61c.
Published:

> (1) 6AA no. 17.
> (2) 6AA bis.
> (3) 6AJ no. 9.

Recorded:

> (1) Folkways FM-3344/5.

x:

> (1) Would I were in Grantchester . . .

G78 The greatest man.

　　Voice & piano (Anne Timoney Collins).

　　1921; 6B69.

　　Published:

　　　　(1) 6AA no. 19.

　　　　(2) 6AA bis.

　　　　(3) 6AC no. 7.

　　　　(4) 6AL no. 1.

　　　　(5) Arrow (Associated Music Publishers), 1939, 1942.

　　Recorded:

　　　　(1) NMQR-1412.

　　　　(2) Nonesuch H-71209st.

　　　　(3) Overtone LP-7.

　　x:

　　　　(1) My teacher said . . .

The greatest of these is liberty.

　　see: The things our fathers loved.

G79 Greek fugue in four keys, string quartet.

　　1897 (?); 2B5.

　　Notes: Unfinished.

　　x:

　　　　(1) Fugue in four keys.

　　　　(2) Fugue, string quartet, 2B5.

Grove, rove, night, delight . . .

　　see: Romanzo di Central Park.

Gup the blood or hearst.

　　see: Set, orchestra, no. 2, 1C32.

Guten Abend . . .

　　see: Wiegenlied.

H19 Hallowe'en.

   Piano & string quartet.

   1907 (?); 2B13.

   Published:

   > (1) Bomart, 1949; published under title Outdoor
   > scenes.

   Recorded:

   > (1) Cambridge 804; CRS-1804st.
   > (2) Composers Recordings Inc. CRI-163.
   > (3) Polymusic PRLP-1001, under title Pieces for
   > orchestra.
   > (4) Vanguard C-10032/4; VCS-10032/4st.

   x:

   > (1) Pieces for orchestra.
   > (2) Outdoor scenes.

H29 Harpalus.

   Voice & piano (Thomas Percy).

   1902; 6B40b.

   Published:

   > (1) 6AA no. 73.
   > (2) 6AC no. 26.

   Recorded:

   > (1) Concert Hall CHC-7.
   > (2) Overtone LP-7.

   x:

   > (1) Oh, Harpalus! . . .

The harvest dawn is near . . .

   see: Harvest home chorales.

Harvest home.

   see: Harvest home chorales.

H33 Harvest home chorales.

SATB, organ, double bass & brasses (George Burgess, John Hampton Gurney & Henry Alford).

1898–1912 (?); 5B2.

Contents: (1) Harvest home.—(2) Lord of the harvest.— (3) Harvest Home.

Published:

(1) Mercury, 1949; (MC 446); pl. no. C-5, C-6, C-7; published collectively, edited by Henry Cowell.

Recorded:

(1) RCA Victor LM-2676; LSC-2676st.

(2) Music Library MLR-7071; contains no. 3 only.

(3) Columbia ML-6321.

x:

(1) Harvest home.

(2) Lord of the harvest.

(3) The harvest dawn is near . . .

(4) Come, ye thankful people . . .

H34 Has she need of monarch's swaying wand . . .

Voice & piano.

1893 (?); 6B18b.

Notes: Kirkpatrick cites title as My Lou Jeninne.

x:

(1) My Lou Jeninne.

H39 Hawthorne overture.

Orchestra.

1910 (?); 1B5/3.

Notes: No. 4 (?) of Men of literature overtures; lost.

x:

(1) Men of literature overtures.

He grew in those seasons . . .

see: Thoreau.

H43 He is there! May 30, 1917, chorus & orchestra.
      (Charles E. Ives)
      1917; 5B11.
   x:
         (1) Fifteen years ago today . . .
         (2) May 30, 1917.

H44 He is there! May 30, 1917, voice & piano.
      (Charles E. Ives).
      1917; 6B57.
      Notes: Subsequently revised as They are there!
      Published:
         (1) 6AA no. 50.
      Recorded:
         (1) Overtone LP-7.
   x:
         (1) Fifteen years ago today . . .
         (2) May 30, 1917.
   sa:
         (1) They are there!

H45 Hear my prayer, O Lord.
      Voice & piano (Nahum Tate & Nicholas Brady).
      1888 (?); 6B10a.
      Published:
         (1) 6AA no. 89.
         (2) 6AH no. 1.
   x:
         (1) O have mercy, Lord . . .

   Heart-shaped yellow leaves . . .
      see: Yellow leaves.

H47 Hell's bells.
   Fraternity show for Delta Kappa Epsilon.
   1896; 4A4.
   Notes: Lost.
   x:
      (1) Delta Kappa Epsilon show, 4A4, Hell's bells.

   Her eyes are like unfathomable lakes . . .
   see: Like unfathomable lakes.

H53 Her gown was of vermilion silk.
   Voice & piano.
   1897 (?); 6B26.

   Here are things . . .
   see: The one way.

H67 His exaltation.
   Low voice & piano (Robert Robinson).
   1913; 6B48c.
   Published:
      (1) 6AA no. 46.
      (2) 6AJ no. 7.
      (3) Sacred songs.
   x:
      (1) For the grandeur of thy nature . . .

H72 Holder klingt der Vogelsang . . .
   Voice & piano (Ludwig Hölty).
   1892; 6B14a.
   Published:
      (1) 6Ab no. 6.

H73 Holiday quickstep, band.
      1888 (?); 1D3.
      Notes: Lost.

H74 Holiday quickstep, orchestra.
   1887; 1C1.
   Notes: Arranged by George Ives.

H75 Holidays.
   Orchestra.
   1904–1913; 1A4.
   Alternate title: A symphony, or New England holidays.
   Contents: (1) Washington's Birthday.—(2) Decoration
   Day.—(3) The Fourth of July.—(4) Thanksgiving
   and/or Forefather's Day.
   Published:
     (1) New Music (Associated Music Publishers), 1936
       (Orchestra series, 20); on rental, contains
       no. 1 only; M60-2455.
     (2) Peer, 196–; on rental, contains no. 2 only.
     (3) New Music (Associated Music Publishers), 1932,
       v.1 (Orchestra series, 3); on rental, contains
       no. 3 only; M60-2464.
     (4) Peer, 196–; on rental, contains no. 4 only.
   Recorded:
     (1) NMQR-1013; contains no. 1 only.
     (2) Composers Recordings Inc. CRI-163; contains
       no. 1 only.
     (3) LOU-621; contains no. 2 only.
     (4) Composers Recordings Inc. CRI-180; contains
       no. 3 only.
     (5) Composers Recordings Inc. CRI-177; contains
       no. 4 only.
     (6) Composers Recordings Inc. CRI-190; 190SDst.
     (7) Columbia MS-7147st.
     (8) Turnabout TV-34146Sst.
     (9) Columbia ML-6243; contains no. 2 only.

(10) Columbia ML-6289; contains no. 3 only.
(11) Columbia ML-6415; contains no. 1 only.
x:

    (1) A symphony: Holidays.
    (2) New England holidays.
    (3) Washington's Birthday.
    (4) Decoration Day.
    (5) The Fourth of July.
    (6) Thanksgiving Day.
    (7) Forefather's Day.

The hope I dreamed of . . .
    see: Mirage.

H82 The Housatonic at Stockbridge.
    Voice & piano (Robert Underwood Johnson).
    1921; 6B64d.
    Published:

    (1) 6AA no. 15.
    (2) 6AG no. 11.
x:

    (1) Contented river . . .
sa:

    (1) Three places in New England.

How can I turn . . .
    see: Tolerance.

How oft a cloud . . .
    see: A night thought.

Hush thee, dear child . . .
    see: Cradle song.

H97 Hymn, 5C1.
    Chorus (textless).
    1887.

Alternate title: First hymn, op. 2, no. 1.
x:
(1) First hymn.

H98 Hymn, 6B62.
Voice & piano (Gerhardt Tersteegen; John Wesley, trans.).
1921.
Published:
(1) 6AA no. 20.
(2) 6AA bis.
(3) 6AC no. 25.
Recorded:
(1) Yaddo I-2.
x:
(1) Thou hidden love of God . . .
sa:
(1) Set, bass & piano quintet.

Hymn, strings; arr.
see: Set, bass & piano quintet.

H99 Hymn anthem on Abide with me.
Chorus.
ca. 1902; 5C39.
Notes: Lost.
sa:
(1) Abide with me.

I closed and drew . . .
see: Slugging a vampire.

I dream of thee . . .
see: Through night and day.

I11 I hear a tone so wondrous rare . . .
   Voice & piano (Peter Cornelius; Hugo Laubach, trans.)
   1895 (?); 6B21b.
   x:
        (1) Mir klingt ein Ton . . .

I12 I knew and loved a maid . . .
   Voice & piano.
   1898 or 1899 (?); 6B30b.

  I know not if thee love . . .
   see: God bless and keep thee.

  I looked into the midnight deep . . .
   see: In my beloved's eyes.

  I sometimes sit beneath a tree . . .
   see: The last reader.

I13 I think of thee, my God.
   Chorus (John S. B. Monsell).
   1899 or 1890 (?); 5C10.

  I think there must be a place . . .
   see: The things our fathers loved.

I14 I travelled among unknown men.
   Medium voice & piano (William Wordsworth).
   1901; 6B37.
   Published:
        (1) 6AA no. 75.
        (2) 6AA bis.
        (3) 6AF no. 9.

I15 I went along the road.
   Voice & piano (D. von Liliencron; John Bernhoff, trans.).
   1899 (?); 6B34a.

I16 I wrote a rhyme . . .
Solo voice & TTBB.
1895 (?); 5D6.
Alternate title: Partsong in A major.
Notes: Lost.
x:
(1) Partsong, 5D6, A major.

I17 Ich grolle nicht.
Voice & piano (Heinrich Heine).
1898; 6B27a.
Published:
(1) 6AA no. 83.
(2) 6AC no. 30.
Recorded:
(1) Society of Participating Artists SPA-9, as
I'll not complain.
(2) Cambridge 804; CRS-1804st.
x:
(1) I'll not complain.

I18 Ich konnte heute nicht schlafen.
Voice & piano (Christian Winther; Edmund Lobedanz,
trans.)
1900 (?); 6B35c.

Ich ruhe still . . .
see: In summer fields.

I'll not complain.
see: Ich grolle nicht.

I29 Ilmenau: Over all the treetops.
Voice & piano (Wolfgang von Goethe; Harmony T. Ives,
trans.).
1902; 6B39a.

Published:
  (1) 6AA no. 68.
  (2) 6AA bis.
  (3) Peer, 1952.
x:
  (1) Over all the treetops . . .
  (2) Über allen Gipfeln ist Ruh . . .

I33 Immortality.
  Voice & piano (Charles E. Ives).
  1921; 6B67a.
  Published:
    (1) 6AA no. 5.
    (2) 6AA bis.
    (3) 6AC no. 5.
  Recorded:
    (1) Folkways 3344/5.
  x:
    (1) Who dares to say . . .

I35 In a mountain spring.
  Voice & piano.
  1891 (?); 6B13b.
  Notes: Lost (?).

I36 In April tide.
  Voice & piano (Clinton Scollard).
  1895 (?); 6B21d.
  x:
    (1) Be ye in love . . .

I37 In autumn.
  Voice & piano.
  1893 (?); 6B18a.

Published:
>> (1) 6Ac no. 20 (?).

x:
>> (1) The skies seemed true . . .

I38 In Flanders field.
Voice & piano (John McCrae).
1917; 6B56.
Notes: Cowell lists this as the third of Three songs of the
First World War, on a text by McRae [sic].
Published:
>> (1) 6AA no. 49.
>> (2) 6AH no. 13.
Recorded:
>> (1) Overtone LP-7.
x:
>> (1) Songs of the First World War.

I39 In my beloved's eyes.
Voice & piano (W. M. Chauvenet).
1895 (?); 6B22e.
x:
>> (1) I looked into the midnight deep . . .

I41 In re con moto et al.
Piano quintet.
1913; 2B18.
Published:
>> (1) Peer, 1968; pl. no. 1078-18; score & parts
>> included; 68-129364/M.

I42 In summer fields.
Voice & piano (Hermann Allmers; Chapman, trans.).
1897; 6B27.
Alternate title: Feldeinsamkeit.

Published:

    (1) 6AA no. 82.

    (2) 6AA bis.

    (3) 6AD no. 19.

Recorded:

    (1) Society of Participating Artists SPA-9.

x:

    (1) Feldeinsamkeit.

    (2) Ich ruhe still . . .

    (3) Quite still I lie . . .

I43 In the alley.

    Voice & piano (Charles E. Ives).

    1896; 6B23d.

    Published:

        (1) 6AA no. 53.

        (2) 6AK no. 4.

    x:

        (1) On my way to work one day . . .

In the barn.

    see: Sonata, violin & piano, no. 2.

In the cage.

    see: Set for theatre or chamber orchestra.

In the inn.

    see: Set for theatre or chamber orchestra.

        Sonata, piano, no. 1.

I44 In the mornin'.

    Voice & piano (Negro spiritual).

    1929; 6B78.

    Published:

        (1) Songs and harmonizations.

In the night.
see: Set for theatre or chamber orchestra.

In these United States.
see: Set of overtures.

I45 Incantation.
Voice & piano (Lord Byron).
1921; 6B62b.
Published:
    (1) 6AA no. 18.
    (2) 6AC no. 8.
x:
    (1) From the incantation.
sa:
    (1) When the moon is on the wave.

I46 The Indians.
Voice & piano (Charles Sprague).
1921; 6B63.
Published:
    (1) 6AA no. 4.
    (2) 6AA bis.
    (3) 6AB no. 3.
Recorded:
    (1) Cambridge 804.
x:
    (1) Alas! for them their day is o'er . . .
sa:
    (1) Set, orchestra, no. 2, 1C32.
    (2) Set, orchestra, no. 5, 1C37.
    (3) Set, orchestra, no. 6, 1C38.

I58 The innate.
     Voice & piano (Charles E. Ives).
     1916; 6B55.
     Published:
          (1) 6AA no. 40.
          (2) 6AD no. 9.
          (3) 6Ae no. 2.
     x:
          (1) Voices live in every finite being . . .
     sa:
          (1) Set, bass & piano quintet.

I61 Intercollegiate march, band.
     1892 (?); 1D5.
     Published:
          (1) Pepper & Co., 1896.
     x:
          (1) March, band, 1D5, no. 5.
          (2) March intercollegiate.

I612 Intercollegiate march, band; arr., orchestra.
      Notes: Arranged by Bernard Hermann (?).—Parts in
      CBS Library.

I62 Interlude for hymns, organ.
     1892 (?); 3D6.

I63 Invention, piano, 3B14, D major.
     1896 (?); 3B14.
     Notes: Title from Kirkpatrick.

   Is that Mr. Reilly . . .
     see: The side show.

   It strikes me that . . .
     see: An election.

J'attends, hélas . . .
  see: Rosamunde.

Jerusalem the golden.
  see: Fantasia on Jerusalem the golden, band.
    Variations on Jerusalem the golden, organ.

J65 Johnny Poe.
  Chorus & orchestra (Benjamin R. C. Low).
  1925; 5B13.
  Notes: Unfinished or lost (?).
  x:
      (1) When fell the gloom . . .

J93 The judgement hall.
  Opera.
  1907 (projected only); 4B2.
  Alternate title: Kimash hills.
  x:
      (1) Kimash hills.

J94 Judges' walk.
  Voice & piano (Arthur Symond).
  1893–1898 (?); 6B28a.
  x:
      (1) That night on Judges' walk . . .

K11 Kären.
  Voice & piano (Parmo Karl Ploug; Clara Kappey, trans.).
  1894 (?); 6B22a.
  Alternate title: Little Kären.
  Published:
      (1) 6AA no. 91.
      (2) 6AA bis.
      (3) 6AG no. 1.

x:
(1) Little Kären.
(2) Do'st remember child . . .

Keats' Like a sick eagle.
see: Like a sick eagle.

Kimash hills.
see: The judgment hall.

K99 Kyrie eleison.
Chorus.
1897 (?); 5C28.
Notes: Lost or unfinished?

Largo: The Indians.
see: Set, orchestra, no. 2, 1C32.

L31 Largo, piano, clarinet & violin.
1901–1902; 2B8.
Published:
(1) Southern, 1953; 54-1539.
Recorded:
(1) Polymusic PRLP-1001.
(2) Sheffield 3; S-3st.
sa:
(1) Trio, piano, clarinet & violin.

L32 Largo, violin & piano.
Not in Kirkpatrick.
Notes: This movement is taken from sketches for the
Pre-no. 1 violin sonata (S748).
Published:
(1) Southern, 1967; Paul Zukofsky, ed.;
67-123051/M.

Largo molto.
see: Like a sick eagle, orchestra.

L33 Largo risoluto, piano quintet, no. 1.
1906 (?); 2B14.
Alternate title: The law of diminishing returns.
Published:
(1) Peer, 1961; pl. no. 583; M61-1188.
x:
(1) The law of diminishing returns.

L34 Largo risoluto, piano quintet, no. 2.
1908 (?); 2B15.
Alternate title: A shadow made—a silhouette.
Published:
(1) Peer, 1961; pl. no. 598-3; M61-1977.
x:
(1) A shadow made—a silhouette.

Largo to presto: The unanswered question.
see: Set, orchestra, no. 4, 1C36.

L35 The lark will make her hymn . . .
Voice & piano (Rudyard Kipling).
1898 (?); 6B28b.

Last, for December . . .
see: December.

L36 The last reader, voice & chamber orchestra.
Notes: Cited in *Composers of the Americas* as written
in 1911; not in Kirkpatrick.

L37 The last reader, voice & piano.
(Oliver Wendell Holmes).
1921; 6B26c.
Published:
(1) 6AA no. 3.
(2) 6AA bis.
(3) 6AC no. 20.

Recorded:
>   (1) Yaddo I-2.

x:
>   (1) I sometimes sit beneath a tree . . .

sa:
>   (1) Set, orchestra, no. 2, 1C32.
>   (2) Set, orchestra, no. 4, 1C36.

The law of diminishing returns.
see: Largo risoluto, piano quintet, no. 1.

L47 A lecture.
Orchestra.
1907 (?); 1C31/ii.
Notes: No. 2 of Set, orchestra, no. 1, 1C31.
x:
>   (1) Set, orchestra, no. 1, 1C31.

L53 Leise zieht durch mein Gemüth . . .
Voice & piano (Heinrich Heine).
1895 (?); 6B22b.

A leopard went around his cage . . .
see: The cage.

L64 Let there be light.
SATB, TTBB, trombones, violins, organ or string orchestra
>   (John Ellerton).
1901; 5C38.
Published:
>   (1) Peer, 1967, 1955; pl. no. 592-1 [parts], 592-2
>   [score]; 67-123056/M.

x:
>   (1) This is the day of light . . .
>   (2) Processional.

L65 Let there be light, men's voices & organ.
Published:
(1) Peer, 1955; pl. no. 311-2.

L66 Let there be light, mixed voices & organ.
Published:
(1) Peer, 1955; pl. no. 312-2.

L72 Life of the world.
Chorus (Ray Palmer, trans., from *Salve mundi salutare*).
1893 (?); 5C20.
Notes: Incomplete; lost or unfinished (?).
sa:
(1) All-forgiving.

A light low in the East . . .
see: Sunrise.

L73 The light that is felt.
Vocal quartet, chorus & organ (John Greenleaf Whittier).
1895.

L74 The light that is felt, voice & piano.
Medium voice & piano (John Greenleaf Whittier).
1904; 6B32.
Published:
(1) 6AA no. 66.
(2) 6AA bis.
(3) Mercury (Presser), 1950.
x:
(1) A tender child of summers . . .

L75 Light-winged smoke.
Voice & piano (H. D. Thoreau).
1914 or 1915 (?); 6B51b.

L76 Like a sick eagle, orchestra.
Unison voices (ad lib.) & orchestra (John Keats).
ca. 1908; 1C31/iv.
Alternate title: Largo molto.
Notes: No. 4 of Set, orchestra, no. 1, 1C31, and no. 1 of Set,
orchestra, no. 5, 1C37.
x:
(1) Largo molto.
(2) Keats' Like a sick eagle.
(3) Set, orchestra, no. 1, 1C31.
sa:
(1) Set, orchestra, no. 5, 1C37.

L77 Like a sick eagle, voice & piano.
(John Keats).
1909 or 1920 (?); 6B45a.
Published:
(1) 6AA no. 26.
(2) 6AA bis.
(3) 6AC no. 22.
Recorded:
(1) Folkways FM-3344/5.

L78 Like unfathomable lakes.
Voice & piano.
1892; 6B15b.
x:
(1) Her eyes are like unfathomable lakes . . .

L81 Lincoln, the great commoner.
SATB, SSAA or TTBB & orchestra (Edwin Markham).
1912; 5B5.
Duration: 4'.

Published:

> (1) New Music, 1932 (Orchestra series, no. 1);
> reprinted in v.26, no. 2, January 1953
> with Presser imprint.

x:

> (1) And so he came . . .
> (2) From "Lincoln, the great commoner."

L82 Lincoln, the great commoner, voice & piano.
(Edwin Markham).
1921; 6B49d.
Published:

> (1) 6AA no. 11.
> (2) Peer, 1952.

Recorded:

> (1) Folkways FM-3344/5.

x:

> (1) And so he came . . .
> (2) From "Lincoln, the great commoner."

Little Kären.
see: Kären.

Little star of Bethlehem.
see: A Christmas carol.

Lord, thou hast been our dwelling place . . .
see: Psalm 90.

L86 Lord God, thy sea is mighty . . .
Chorus.
1893 or 1894 (?); 5C21.

The Lord is my shepherd . . .
see: Psalm 23.

Lord of the harvest.
see: Harvest home chorales.

The lotos flow'r is drooping . . .
see: Die Lotosblume.

L88 Die Lotosblume.
Voice & piano (Heinrich Heine).
1899 (?); 6B22c.
Published:
(1) 6AA no. 97.
(2) 6AC no. 29.
x:
(1) The lotos flow'r is drooping . . .

L91 Love divine.
Voice & piano (Oliver Wendell Holmes).
1898 (?); 6B30a.
x:
(1) O love divine . . .

L92 Love does not die.
Soprano or tenor & piano.
1894 or 1895 (?); 5D4.

The love song of Har Dyal.
see: Alone upon the housetops . . .

Low lie the mists . . .
see: Mists.

L94 Luck and work.
Voice & piano (Robert Underwood Johnson).
1920 (?); 6B45b.
Published:
(1) 6AA no. 21.
(2) 6AA bis.

      (3) 6AE no. 4.

      (4) 6AC no. 12.

x:

      (1) While one will search . . .

sa:

      (1) Set, orchestra, no. 3, 1C35.

      (2) Set, orchestra, no. 5, 1C37.

M19 Magnificat.
Voice & piano (St. Luke).
1892 (?); 6B15c.
x:

      (1) My soul doth magnify the Lord.

M23 Major Andre overture.
Orchestra (to play by Judge Lyman D. Brewster).
1903–1904; 4B1.

M24 The majority.
Chorus & orchestra (Charles E. Ives).
1914; 5B10.
Alternate title: The masses.
x:

      (1) The masses have toiled.

M25 The majority, voice & piano.
(Charles E. Ives).
1921; 6B65.
Published:

      (1) 6AA no. 1.

      (2) 6AD no. 16.

Recorded:

      (1) Folkways 3344/5.

x:

      (1) The masses have toiled . . .

Make a joyful noise unto the Lord . . .
see: Psalm 100.

Man passes down the way of years . . .
see: The all-enduring.

M29 Maple leaves.
Voice & piano (Thomas Bailey Aldrich).
1920; 6B61e.
Published:
(1) 6AA no. 23.
(2) 6AB no. 4.
Recorded:
(1) Folkways 3344/5.
(2) Overtone LP-7.
x:
(1) October turned my maple leaves to gold . . .

March, band, 1D5, no. 5.
see: Intercollegiate march, band.

M31 March, band, 1D6, C & F.
1896.

M321 March, orchestra, 1C3, no. 1.
1890 (?).
Notes: Lost.

M322 March, orchestra, 1C4, no. 2, B flat & F.
1892 or 1895 (?).
Alternate title: Rim II.
x:
(1) Rim II.

M323 March, orchestra, 1C5, no. 3, C & F.
1892 or 1893 (?).

M324 March, orchestra, 1C6, no. 3.
    1892, 1893 or 1894 (?).
    Alternate title: Rim III.
    x:
       (1) Rim III.

M325 March, orchestra, 1C7, no. 4, C & F.
    1892, 1893 or 1894 (?).

M326 March, orchestra, 1C9, no. 6.
    1896 or 1897 (?).
    Notes: Lost.

M331 March, piano, 3B4, no. 1, B flat & F.
    1890 (?).

M332 March, piano, 3B5, no. 2, C & F.
    1892 (?).

M333 March, piano, 3B6, no. 3, C & F.
    1892 (?).

M334 March, piano, 3B7, no. 3a.
    1892 or 1893 (?).
    Notes: Lost (?).

M335 March, piano, 3B8, no. 3b.
    1892, 1893 or 1894 (?).
    Notes: Lost (?).

M336 March, piano, 3B9, no. 4.
    1892, 1893 or 1894 (?).
    Notes: Lost (?).

M337 March, piano, 3B10, no. 5, B flat & D.
    1892 (?).

M338 March, piano, 3B11, no. 5a, C & G.
1893.

M339 March, piano, 3B13, no. 6, D & G.
1895–1896 (?).

March: The circus band.
see: Circus band, orchestra.
Circus band, piano.

M34 March for Dewey Day, band.
1899; 1D8.
Notes: Lost.

March intercollegiate, band.
see: Intercollegiate march, band.

M35 Marie.
Voice & piano (Gottschall; Elisabeth Rücker, trans.).
1896; 6B23b.
Published:
(1) 6AA no. 92.
(2) 6AA bis.
(3) 6Ab no. 5.
(4) 6AH no. 3.
x:
(1) Marie, am Fenster sitzest du . . .
(2) Marie, I see thee . . .

Marie, am Fenster sitzest du . . .
see: Marie.

Marie, I see thee . . .
see: Marie.

The masses have toiled . . .
see: The majority.

M43 Matthew Arnold overture.
Orchestra.
1912; 1B5/4.
Notes: No. 3 of Men of literature overtures.—Mostly lost.
x:
> (1) Men of literature overtures.
> (2) Arnold overture.

May 30, 1917.
see: He is there! May 30, 1917.

M52 Melody, organ, 3D9, E flat.
1890 or 1893 (?).
Notes: Unfinished or lost (?).—Title from Kirkpatrick.

M53 Memorial slow march, organ.
1901; 3D22.
Notes: Lost.

M54 Memories.
Medium voice & piano (Charles E. Ives).
1897; 6B26a.
Contents: (1) Very pleasant.—(2) Rather sad.
Published:
> (1) 6AA no. 102.
> (2) 6AF no. 6.

x:
> (1) We're sitting in the opera house . . .

Men of literature overtures.
see: Emerson overture.
> Robert Browning overture.
> Matthew Arnold overture.
> Hawthorne overture.

Mike Donlin—Johnny Evers.
see: Set of cartoons or take-offs.

M66 Minuet, piano, op. 4.
    1886; 3B1.

  Mir klingt ein Ton . . .
    see: I hear a tone so wondrous rare . . .

M67 Mirage.
    Medium voice & piano (Christina Rossetti).
    1902; 6B41.
    Published:
        (1) 6AA no. 70.
        (2) 6AA bis.
        (3) 6AF no. 10.
    Recorded:
        (1) Concert Hall CHC-7.
    x:
        (1) The hope I dreamed of . . .

M68 Mists, 6B47.
    Voice & piano (Harmony T. Ives)
    1910.
    x:
        (1) Low lie the mists . . .

M69 Mists, 6B47a.
    Voice & piano (Harmony T. Ives).
    1910.
    Published:
        (1) 6AA no. 57.
        (2) 6AA bis.
        (3) 6AC no. 21.
    Recorded:
        (1) Concert Hall CHC-7.
        (2) Folkways FM-3344/5.
        (3) Society of Participating Artists SPA-9.

x:

(1) Low lie the mists . . .

M86 Morning service.
Chorus.
1893–1894 (?)
Notes: Lost.

The mountain stirred its bushy crown . . .
see: Amphion.

My dear old mother . . .
see: The old mother, 6B36b.

My heart leaps up when I behold . . .
see: The rainbow, voice & piano.

M96 My life has grown so dear to me . . .
Voice & piano.
1899 (?); 6B32a.

My Lou Jeninne.
see: Has she need of monarch's swaying wand . . .

M97 My native land, 6B21f.
Voice & piano (trans. from Heinrich Heine).
1895.
Alternate title: Un rêve.
Published:

(1) 6AA no. 101.
(2) 6AG no. 3.

x:

(1) Un rêve.

M98 My native land, 6B38c.
Voice & piano (trans. from Heinrich Heine).
1901 (?).

Published:
> (1) 6Ac no. 19 (?).

x:
> (1) Un rêve.

My soul doth magnify the Lord . . .
see: Magnificat.

M99 My sweet Jeannette.
TTBB.
1898 (?); 5D13.
Notes: Lost or unfinished (?).

My teacher said . . .
see: The greatest man.

Nascentes morimur.
see: Slants, or Christian and pagan.

Nature's relentless . . .
see: On the antipodes.

N31 Nature's way.
Voice & piano (Charles E. Ives).
1908; 6B44b.
Published:
> (1) 6AA no. 61.
> (2) 6AA bis.
> (3) 6AH no. 10.

x:
> (1) When the distant evening bell . . .

Naught that country needeth . . .
see: The celestial country. Naught that country needeth.

N35 'Neath the elm trees . . .
TTBB.
1895 (?); 5D5.

New England holidays.
see: Holidays.
Sonata, violin & piano, no. 5.

A New England symphony.
see: Three places in New England.

N53 The new river.
Mixed voices & chamber orchestra (Charles E. Ives).
1907 (?); 5B4.
Alternate title: The ruined river.
Published:
(1) Peer, 196–; ed. by Henry Cowell.
Recorded:
(1) Columbia ML-6321.
x:
(1) Down the river comes a noise . . .
sa:
(1) The ruined river.
(2) Set, orchestra, no. 6, 1C38.

N54 The new river, voice & piano.
(Charles E. Ives).
1921; 6B49.
Published:
(1) 6AA no. 6.
(2) 6AA bis.
(3) 6AC no. 19.
(4) Peer, 196–
x:
(1) Down the river comes a noise . . .

N55 New year's dance, piano.
1887; 3B2.

N67 Night of frost in May.
   Voice & piano (George Meredith).
   1899; 6B34.
   Published:
       (1) 6AA no. 84.
       (2) 6AA bis.
       (3) 6AD no. 13.
   Recorded:
       (1) Concert Hall CHC-7.
   x:
       (1) There was the lyre of earth . . .

N68 A night song.
   Voice & piano (Thomas Moore).
   1895; 6B21.
   Published:
       (1) 6AA no. 88.
       (2) Peer, 1952.
   Recorded:
       (1) Concert Hall CHC-7.
   x:
       (1) The young May soon . . .

N69 A night song; arr., orchestra.
   Notes: Arranged by Amadeo di Filippi in 1943.

N71 A night thought.
   Voice & piano (Thomas Moore).
   1895 (?); 6B41c.
   Published:
       (1) 6AA no. 107.
       (2) 6AA bis.
       (3) 6AC no. 31.

Recorded:

(1) Society of Participating Artists SPA-9.

x:

(1) How oft a cloud . . .

Ninety-six.
see: Romanzo di Central Park.

N73 No more.
Voice & piano (William Winter).
1897; 6B28.
Published:

(1) Songs and harmonizations.

x:

(1) They walked beside the summer sea . . .

Not only in my lady's eyes.
see: Canon: Not only in my lady's eyes.

November 2, 1920.
see: An election.

Now came still evening . . .
see: Evening.

Now help us, Lord . . .
see: The collection.

O11 O breath of early morning . . .
Voice & piano (Huntington Mason).
1898 (?); 6B29.

O12 O danke nicht für diese Lieder . . .
Voice & piano (Wilhelm Müller).
1897 (?); 6B26b.

O doux printemps . . .
see: Elégie.

O13 O God, my heart is fixed.
Chorus (Psalm 108/1; Nahum Tate & Nicolas Brady, trans.).
1892; 5C17.
Notes: Unfinished or lost (?).
x: Psalm 108, v. 1.

O have mercy, Lord . . .
see: Hear my prayer, O Lord.

O love divine . . .
see: Love divine.

O14 O maiden fair.
Baritone solo, TTBB & piano.
1898; 5D12.

O Sabbath rest of Galilee . . .
see: Serenity.

O turn ye . . .
see: Turn ye, turn ye.

October turned my maple leaves to gold . . .
see: Maple leaves.

O'er the mountain . . .
see: Berceuse.

Oh dearest mother . . .
see: The old mother.

Oh, Harpalus! . . .
see: Harpalus.

Oh sunny days . . .
see: Two little flowers.

Oh, the days are gone . . .
see: Canon: Oh, the days are gone.

O43 An old flame.
    Voice & piano (Charles E. Ives).
    1896; 6B23c.
    Alternate title: A retrospect.
    Published:
        (1) 6AA no. 87.
        (2) 6AK no. 3.
        (3) 6Ac no. 17 (?).
    x:
        (1) Where dreams enfold me . . .
        (2) A retrospect.

O44 Old home day.
    Voice & piano (Charles E. Ives, after Virgil).
    1920 (?); 6B49e.
    Published:
        (1) 6AA no. 52.
        (2) 6AA bis.
        (3) 6AK no. 13.
    x:
        (1) Go, my songs! . . .

An old man with a straw . . .
    see: The see'r.

O45 The old mother, 6B20a.
    Voice & piano (A. O. Vinje; Frederick Corder, trans).
    1894 (?).
    Published:
        (1) 6 Ac no. 25 (?).
    x:
        (1) Oh dearest mother . . .

O46 The old mother, 6B36b.
      Voice & piano (A. O. Vinje; Edmund Lodedanz &
        Frederick Corder, trans.).
      1900.
      Published:
            (1) 6AA no. 81.
            (2) 6AK no. 8.
      x:
            (1) Du alte Mutter . . .
            (2) My dear old mother . . .

O47 An old song deranged.
      Instrumental ensemble.
      1903 (?); 2B10.

O55 Omens and oracles.
      Medium voice & piano.
      1900; 6B35.
      Published:
            (1) 6AA no. 86.
            (2) 6AF no. 8.
      x:
            (1) Phantoms of the future . . .

      On my way to work one day . . .
        see: In the alley.

      On shining shore.
        see: Fugue, string quartet, 2B4.

O57 On the antipodes.
      Voice or chorus & 2 pianos or organs (Charles E. Ives).
      1915–1923; 6B17.
      Published:
            (1) 6AD no. 18.

Recorded:

    (1) Folkways 3344/5.

x:

    (1) Nature's relentless . . .

O59 On the counter.
    Voice & piano (Charles E. Ives).
    1920; 6B61d.
    Published:

        (1) 6AA no. 28.
        (2) 6AH no. 14.

    x:

        (1) Tunes we heard in ninety-two . . .

O61 One, two, three.
    Voice & piano (Charles E. Ives).
    1921; 6B66a.
    Published:

        (1) 6AA no. 41.
        (2) 6AE no. 3.

    Recorded:

        (1) Cambridge 804; CRS-1804st.
        (2) Concert Hall CHC-7.
        (3) Overtone LP-7.

    x:

        (1) Why doesn't one, two, three . . .

One evening just at sunset . . .
    see: Slow march.

O62 The one way.
    Voice & piano (Charles E. Ives).
    1923 (?); 6B72.

Published:

 (1) Songs and harmonizations.

x:

 (1) Here are things . . .

O64 Orchard House overture.

 Orchestra.

 1904; 1C19.

 Notes: Lost.

 Orchestral set, no. 1.

 see: Three places in New England.

O65 Orchestral set, no. 2.

 1912–1915; 1A6.

 Contents: (1) An elegy to our forefathers.—(2) The
 rockstrewn hills join in the people's outdoor meeting.—
 (3) From Hanover Square north, at the end of a tragic
 day, the voice of the people again arose.

 Published:

  (1) Peer, 196-; rental.

 Recorded:

  (1) RCA Victor LM-2959; LSC-2959st.

 x:

  (1) An elegy to our forefathers.

  (2) The rockstrewn hills.

  (3) From Hanover Square.

  (4) Set, orchestra, no. 2, 1A6.

O66 Orchestral set, no. 3.

 1919–1926; 1A8.

 Notes: Unfinished.

 Contains three movements.

 x:

  (1) Set, orchestra, no. 3, 1A8.

Outdoor scenes
see: Central Park in the dark.
Hallowe'en.
The pond.

Over all the treetops . . .
see: Ilmenau: Over all the treetops.

O96 Over the pavements.
Winds & piano.
1906–1913; 1C24.
Alternate title: Scherzo, band (Library of Congress).
Published:
(1) Peer, 1954; M56-1136.
Recorded:
(1) Cambridge 804; CRS-1804st.
(2) Polymusic PRLP-1001; under title Pieces for
orchestra.
x:
(1) Scherzo, band.
(2) Scherzo: Over the pavements.
(3) Pieces for orchestra.

Overture: Town, gown and state.
see: Town, gown and state overture.

O97 Overture, orchestra, 1B2, G minor.
1895 or 1896.
Notes: Unfinished or lost (?).

O98 Overture and march "1776," orchestra.
1903–1904; 1C18.
Notes: Kirkpatrick lists sketches for expansion under
1B9 (1914–1915).
sa:
(1) 1776.

P22 Paracelsus.
    Voice & piano (Robert Browning).
    1921; 6B66b.
    Published:
        (1) 6AA no. 30.
        (2) 6AA bis.
        (3) 6AD no. 14.
    Recorded:
        (1) Duke.
        (2) Folkways 3344/5.
    x:
        (1) For God is glorified in man . . .

  Partsong, 5D6, A major.
    see: I wrote a rhyme . . .

P27 Partsong, 5D9, B flat & D.
    TTBB.
    1896 (?).
    Notes: Lost or unfinished?.

P28 Pass the can along.
    Song with chorus (Charles E. Ives).
    1898 or 1897 (?); 4A6.
    Notes: Written for Delta Kappa Epsilon.
    x:
        (1) Fill, fill, fill . . .

P35 Peaks.
    Voice & piano (Henry Bellamann).
    1923 (?); 6B74.
    Published:
        (1) Songs and harmonizations.
    x:
        (1) Quiet faces . . .

People of the world.
see: Sneak thief.

P43 A perfect day.
Voice & piano.
1893 or 1894 (?); 6B18c.
Published:
(1) 6Ac no. 13 (?).
x:
(1) Bland air and leagues . . .

Phantoms of the future . . .
see: Omens and oracles.

P61 Pictures.
Voice & piano (Monica Peveril Turnbull).
1907; 6B42a.
Published:
(1) 6Ab no. 7.
(2) Songs and harmonizations.
x:
(1) The ripe corn bends low . . .

P62 Piece, organ & chamber orchestra, 1C23.
1905 (?).
Notes: Lost.

P63 Pieces, piano, 3B3, G minor.
1889 (?).
Notes: Lost or unfinished.

P64 Pieces, string quartet, 2B1a.
1891.
Notes: Unfinished or lost?—Possibly in G major.

P66 Piece for communion service, organ.
  1901; 3D26.
  Notes: Lost.

P67 Piece on Beautiful river, orchestra.
  1905; 1C22.
  Notes: Lost.
  x:
      (1) Beautiful river.

P68 Piece on Watchman, orchestra.
  1905; 1C21.
  Notes: Unfinished or lost.
  sa:
      (1) Watchman.

  Pieces, basset horn, flute, percussion & 3 violins.
    see: Set, orchestra, no. 3, 1C35.

  Pieces, piano (quarter-tone).
    see: Quarter-tone pieces, piano.

  Pieces, piano & orchestra.
    see: Set for theatre or chamber orchestra.

  Pieces for orchestra.
    see: Central Park in the dark.
      Hallowe'en.
      Over the pavements.
      The unanswered question.

  Poems of Kipling.
    see: Tarrant moss.
      Alone upon the housetops.

P76 Polonaise, 2 cornets & piano.
  1887 (?); 2B1.
  Notes: Incomplete.

P79 The pond.
    Orchestra.
    1906; 1C26.
    Published:
        (1) Bomart, 1949; published under title Outdoor
            scenes.
        (2) Associated Music Publishers, [n.d.]; rental.
    Recorded:
        (1) Cambridge 809; CRS-1809st.
        (2) Composers Recordings Inc. CRI-162.
    x:
        (1) Outdoor scenes.

  Postlude: Children's Day parade.
    see: Children's Day parade.

P85 Postlude, orchestra, 1B1, F major.
    1895.

P86 Postlude, organ, 3D4, F major.
    1890 or 1892 (?).
    Notes: Lost.

P87 Postlude, organ, 3D12.
    1896.
    Notes: Lost.

P88 Postlude, organ, 3D13.
    1897.
    Notes: Lost.

P89 Postlude for Thanksgiving service, organ.
    1897; 3D18.
    Notes: Lost.

  Praise ye the Lord, praise God . . .
    see: Psalm 150.

Praise ye the Lord, praise ye . . .
see: Psalm 135.

La pregunta incontestada.
see: The unanswered question.

P91 Prelude, organ, 3D10.
1896.
Notes: Lost.

P911 Prelude, organ, 3D11.
1896.
Notes: Lost.

P912 Prelude, organ, 3D23.
1901.
Notes: Lost.

P913 Prelude, organ, 3D24.
1901.
Notes: Lost.

P914 Prelude, violin & piano.
1900; not in Kirkpatrick.
Notes: Manuscript fragment cited in *Composers of the Americas.*

P915 Prelude for Thanksgiving service, organ.
1897; 3D17.
Notes: Lost.

P916 Prelude on Abide with me.
Organ, trombone & 2 violins.
1899 (?); 2B6.
sa:
(1) Abide with me.

P917 Preludes, organ, 3D25.
    1901.
    Notes: Lost.

P918 Premonitions.
    Voice & piano (Robert Underwood Johnson).
    1921; 6B65a.
    Published:
        (1) 6AA no. 24.
        (2) 6AC no. 11.
    x:
        (1) There's a shadow on the grass . . .
    sa:
        (1) Set, orchestra, no. 3, 1C35.

  Processional.
    see: Let there be light.

P96 Protests.
    Piano.
    1910 (?); 3B20.
    Alternate title: Varied air with variations.
    Contents: (1) March time or faster.—(2) Adagio or
      allegro or varied or/and variations, very nice.—
      (3) A canon.
    Published:
        (1) New Music, 1947; v. 21, no. 1.
        (2) Presser, [n.d. ?].
    Recorded:
        (1) Folkways FM-3348.
    x:
        (1) Varied air with variations, piano.

P97 Psalm 14.
  Chorus.
  1899 or 1900 (?); 5C35.
  Published:
      (1) Mercury (?), 195–.
  x:
      (1) The fool hath said in his heart . . .

P971 Psalm 23.
  Chorus.
  1898 or 1899 (?); 5C34.
  Notes: Lost.
  x:
      (1) The Lord is my shepherd . . .

P972 Psalm 24.
  SATB.
  1897 (?); 5C30.
  Published:
      (1) Mercury, 1955 (MC 155-8).
  Recorded:
      (1) Columbia ML-6321.
  x:
      (1) The earth is the Lord's . . .

P973 Psalm 25.
  Chorus.
  1897 (?); 5C29.
  Published:
      (1) Mercury (?), 195–
  x:
      (1) Unto thee, O God . . .

P974 Psalm 42.
    Chorus (Nahum Tate & Nicholas Brady, trans.).
    1885 (or 1887?); 5C3.
    x:
        (1) As pants the hart . . .

P975 Psalm 54.
    Chorus.
    1896 (?); 5C27.
    Published:
        (1) Mercury (?), 195–.
    x:
        (1) Save me, O God . . .

P976 Psalm 67.
    SATB.
    1894–1897; 5C24.
    Published:
        (1) Arrow (Associated Music Publishers), 1939;
            pl. no. AMP A274.
    Recorded:
        (1) Columbia 17139D.
        (2) New Records NRLP-305.
        (3) Music Library MLR-7071.
        (4) Recorded Publications Co. CC-3.
        (5) Society for the Preservation of the American
            Musical Heritage MTA-116.
    x:
        (1) God be merciful unto us . . .

P977 Psalm 90.
    SATB, bells & organ.
    1898–1901 (?); 5C37.

Published:
>   (1) Presser (?), 196(9?).

x:
>   (1) Lord, thou hast been our dwelling place . . .

P978 Psalm 100.
>   Chorus.
>   1898 or 1899; 5C33.
>   Published:
>   >   (1) Presser, 196(9?).
>
>   x:
>   >   (1) Make a joyful noise unto the Lord . . .

Psalm 108, v. 1.
>   see: O God, my heart is fixed.

Psalm 108, v. 5.
>   see: Be thou, O God, exalted high . . .

P979 Psalm 135.
>   Chorus.
>   1899 or 1900 (?); 5C36.
>   Alternate title: Anthem-processional.
>   Published:
>   >   (1) Mercury (?), 195-.
>
>   x:
>   >   (1) Praise ye the Lord, praise ye . . .
>   >   (2) Anthem-processional.

Psalm 139, v.23-24.
>   see: Search me, O Lord.

P98 Psalm 150.
>   Chorus.
>   1898; 5C26.

Published:

> (1) Presser, 196(9?).

x:

(1) Praise ye the Lord, praise God . . .

Putnam's camp.
> see: Three places in New England.

Quaint name . . .
> see: Ann Street.

Q1 Quarter-tone pieces, piano.
> 1923–1924; 3C3.
> Duration: 10'40".
> Notes: May also be played by 2 pianos, one quarter-tone apart.
> Contents: (1) Largo.—(2) Allegro.—(3) Adagio; chorale.
> Published:
>> (1) [?].
> Recorded:
>> (1) Odyssey 32-16-0161; 32-16-0162st.
> x:
>> (1) Pieces, piano (quarter-tone).

Q11 Quartet, strings, no. 1.
> 1896; 2A1.
> Duration: 23'53".
> Contents: (1) Chorale; andante [subsequently withdrawn].
> —(1a) Prelude; allegro.—(2) Offertory; adagio cantabile.—(3) Postlude; allegro marziale; andante.
> Published:
>> (1) Peer, 1963; pl. no. 724; 63-43151/M.
> Recorded:
>> (1) Vox DL-1120; STDL-501120st.
>> (2) Pye GGC-4104.

(3) CBS 72630.

(4) Columbia ML-6427; MS-7027.

(5) Turnabout TV-39157st.

x:

(1) A revival service.

Q12 Quartet, strings, pre-no. 2.
1905; 2A2.
Notes: Unfinished or lost.

Q2 Quartet, strings, no. 2.
1907–1913; 2A3.
Duration: 21'50"; 24'37".
Contents: (1) Discussions.—(2) Arguments.—(3) The call of the mountains.
Published:
(1) Peer, 1954; pl. no. 293-26; M54-2732.
Recorded:
(1) Period SPLP-501.
(2) Disc 775.
(3) Folkways FM-3369.
(4) Vox DL-1120; STDL-501120st.
(5) Columbia ML-6427; MS-9027st.
(6) CBS 72630.
(7) Turnabout TV-34157st.
x:
(1) Arguments.
(2) The call of the mountains.
(3) Discussions.

Q6 Qu'il m'irait bien.
Voice & piano (Moreau Delano, trans.).
1901 (?); 6B25e.

Published:
>> (1) 6AA no. 76.
>> (2) 6AG no. 4.

Quiet faces . . .
> see: Peaks.

Quite still I lie . . .
> see: In summer fields.

R14 Ragtime dance, orchestra.
> 1902–1903; 1C15.
> Notes: Lost.

R15 The rainbow.
> Medium voice & orchestra (William Wordsworth).
> 1914; 1C33.
> Alternate title: So may it be.
> Published:
>> (1) Peer, 1959; pl. no. 490; M59-1196.
> Recorded:
>> (1) Cambridge 804; CRS-1804st.
> x:
>> (1) So it may be.
>> (2) My heart leaps up when I behold . . .

R16 The rainbow, voice & piano.
> (William Wordsworth).
> 1921; 6B64e.
> Published:
>> (1) 6AA no. 8.
>> (2) 6AC no. 16.

R38 Religion.
> Medium voice & piano (James T. Bixby, after Lizzie York Case).
> 1920; 6B47b.

Published:
>   (1) 6AA no. 16.
>   (2) 6AA bis.
>   (3) 6AG no. 8.
>   (4) Sacred songs.

Recorded:
>   (1) Cambridge 804; CRS-1804st.

sa:
>   (1) There is no unbelief.

R39 Remembrance.
> Voice & piano (Charles E. Ives).
> 1921; 6B62a.
> Published:
>>   (1) 6AA no. 12.
>>   (2) 6AA bis.
>>   (3) 6AG no. 9.
> x:
>>   (1) A sound of distant horn . . .

R42 Requiem, voice & piano.
> (Robert Louis Stevenson).
> 1911; 6B48.
> Published:
>>   (1) 6AD no. 3.
> Recorded:
>>   (1) Folkways 3344/5.
> x:
>>   (1) Under the wide and starry sky . . .

R43 Resolution.
> Voice & piano (Charles E. Ives).
> 1921 (?); 6B68a.

Published:
    (1) 6AA no. 13.
    (2) 6AA bis.
    (3) 6AD no. 17.
Recorded:
    (1) NMQR-1412.
x:
    (1) Walking stronger under distant skies . . .

A retrospect.
   see: An old flame.

Un rêve.
   see: My native land.

The revival.
   see: Sonata, violin & piano, no. 2.

A revival service.
   see: Quartet, strings, no. 1.

Rim II.
   see: March, orchestra, 1C4, no. 2, B flat & F.

Rim III.
   see: March, orchestra, 1C6, no. 3.

Ring out, sweet chime . . .
   see: The bells of Yale.

The ripe corn bends low . . .
   see: Pictures

R64 Robert Browning overture.
    Orchestra.
    1908–1912; 1B5/2.
    Duration: 18'40".
    Notes: No. 2 of Men of literature overture.

Published:
> (1) Peer, 1959; four missing pages recomposed
> by Lou Harrison or Henry Cowell; M59-904.

Recorded:
> (1) Composers Recordings Inc. CRI-196; 196SDst.
> (2) Vanguard VCS-10013st.
> (3) Columbia ML-6415.
> (4) RCA Victor LM-2959; LSC-2959st.

x:
> (1) Browning overture.
> (2) Men of literature overtures.

R68 Rock of ages.
Voice & piano (Augustus M. Toplady).
1890 or 1892 (?); 6B12b.

x:
> (1) Songs and harmonizations.

The rockstrewn hills.
see: Orchestral set, no. 2.

R75 Romanzo di Central Park.
Voice & piano (Leigh Hunt).
1900; 6B36.
Alternate title: Ninety-six.
Published:
> (1) 6AA no. 96.
> (2) 6AH no. 6.

x:
> (1) Ninety-six.
> (2) Grove, rove, night, delight . . .

R78 Rosamunde.
Voice & piano (Wilhelmine von Chézy; Bélanger, trans.).
1898; 6B21a.

Published:
> (1) 6AA no. 79.
> (2) 6AH no. 4.

x:
> (1) J'attends, hélas . . .
> (2) Der voll Mond . . .

R85 Rough wind.
Voice & piano (Percy B. Shelley).
1902; 6B40a.
Published:
> (1) 6AA no. 69.
> (2) 6AC no. 27.
Recorded:
> (1) Concert Hall CHC-7.

Round and round the old dance ground . . .
see: Waltz, voice & piano.

R88 Royal rivals.
Music for Phi Sigma Tau show (Elisha Ely Garrison).
1894; 4A1.
Notes: Lost.

Rube trying to walk 2 or 3.
see: Set of cartoons or take-offs.

R93 The ruined river.
Orchestra.
1907 (?); 1C31/iii.
Alternate title: The new river.
Notes: No. 3 of Set, orchestra, 1C31, no. 1.
x:
> (1) Set, orchestra, no. 1, 1C31.
sa:
> (1) The new river.

R94 Runaway horse on Main Street.
Band.
1905 (?); 1D9,

R95 Runaway horse on Main Street, voice & piano.
(Charles E. Ives).
1909; 6B45d.
x:
(1) So long Harris . . .

S12 Sacred songs.
Voice & piano.
Contents: (1) Abide with me.—(2) The camp meeting.—
(3) The collection.—(4) Disclosure.—(5) Down
east.—(6) Forward into light.—(7) Naught that country
needeth [from The celestial country].—(8) Religion.—
(9) The waiting soul.—(10) Watchman!.—
(11) Where the eagle.
Published:
(1) Peer, 1961; 62-27398/M [publication is under
publisher's title, Sacred songs; Library of Congress
uses title "Songs. Selections"].
x:
(1) Songs, Sacred.
sa:
(1) [titles of contents].

The St. Gaudens.
see: Three places in New England.

Save me, O God . . .
see: Psalm 54.

Scenes from my childhood . . .
see: Tom sails away.

LIBRARY
OKALOOSA - WALTON JUNIOR COLLEGE

Scherzo: All the way around and back.
see: All the way around and back.

Scherzo: Over the pavements.
see: Over the pavements.

Scherzo: The se'er.
see: The se'er.
Set, orchestra, no. 4, 1C36.

Scherzo, band.
see: Over the pavements.

Scherzo, string quartet.
see: Set, bass & piano quintet.

S37 Schoolboy march, band, op. 1.
1886; 1D1.
Notes: Lost.

S42 A Scotch lullaby.
Voice & piano (Charles Edmund Merrill, Jr.).
ca. 1896; 6B24b.
Published:
    (1) A Yale courant, 1896, v.33, no.5, p. 125-127.
    (2) Songs and harmonizations.
x:
    (1) Blaw, skirlin' win' . . .

S43 A sea dirge.
Voice & piano (William Shakespeare).
1925; 6B75.
Published:
    (1) Songs and harmonizations.
x:
    (1) Full fathom five thy father lies . . .

S44 The sea of sleep.
Voice & piano.
1903; 6B41a.
x:

(1) Good night, my care and my sorrow . . .

S45 Search me, O Lord.
Chorus (Psalm 139, v.23-24).
1891–1892 (?); 5C15.
x:

(1) Psalm 129, v.23-24.

S46 The se'er.
Piano, winds & percussion.
1907 (?); 1C31/i.
Notes: No. 1 of Set, orchestra, no. 1, 1C31.
x:

(1) Set, orchestra, no. 1, 1C31.
(2) Scherzo: The se'er.

S47 The se'er, voice & piano.
(Charles E. Ives).
1920 (?); 6B49a.
Published:

(1) 6AA no. 29.
(2) 6AB no. 5.

Recorded:

(1) Overtone LP-7.

x:

(1) An old man with a straw . . .

sa:

(1) Set, orchestra, no. 4, 1C36.

S48 September.
Voice & piano (Folgore da San Geminiano; Dante Gabriel
Rossetti, trans.).
1920; 6B61b.
Published:
(1) 6AA no. 36.
(2) 6AC no. 9.
Recorded:
(1) Folkways FM-3344/5.
x:
(1) And in September . . .

S51 Serenity.
Chorus & orchestra (John Greenleaf Whittier).
ca. 1909; 5B3.
Notes: Lost.
x:
(1) O Sabbath rest of Galilee . . .

S52 Serenity, voice & piano.
Unison voices or solo voice & piano (John Greenleaf
Whittier).
1919; 6B60d.
Published:
(1) 6AA no. 42.
(2) 6AB no. 6.
(3) Arrow, 1939 (Associated Music Publishers, 1942);
pl. no. AMP 96233-2.
Recorded:
(1) Overtone LP-7.
(2) Columbia ML-6321.
(3) Folkways FM-3344/5.
(4) Columbia MS-6921st; arranged for unison voices
& orchestra.

x:

    (1) O Sabbath rest of Galilee . . .

S53 Serenity; arr., chorus & orchestra.
    Notes: Arranged by Amadeo di Filippi, 1943.

S54 Set, bass & piano quintet.
    1903–1908; 2B16.
    Alternate title: Set of three short pieces.
    Notes: Ives indicates "basso" for double bass and for
      bass voice.
    Contents (Kirkpatrick lists tempo indications as movement
      titles): (1) Hymn; largo cantabile.—(2) Scherzo.—
      (3) The innate; adagio cantabile.
    Published:
      (1) Peer, 1966; pl. no. 1060-40; contains Hymn only,
        in score & parts, as "arranged" for string orchestra;
        66-98064/M.
      (2) Peer, 1958; contains Scherzo only, in score & parts,
        as Scherzo for string quartet; M58-1127.
      (3) Peer, 1967; pl. no. 1070-4; published in
        score & parts.
    Recorded:
      (1) Cambridge 804; CRS-1804st.
    x:
      (1) Scherzo, string quartet.
      (2) Hymn, strings.
      (3) Set of three short pieces.
    sa:
      (1) Hymn, 6B62.
      (2) The innate.

S541 Set, bass & piano quintet. Hymn; arr., string orchestra.
    Notes: Arrangement by Bernard Hermann (?), 1938.

Set, orchestra, no. 1, 1A5.
  see: Three places in New England.

Set, orchestra, no. 1, 1C31.
  see: The se'er.
    A lecture.
    The ruined river.
    Like a sick eagle, orchestra.
    Calcium light night (1898–1907).
    When the moon is on the wave.
    Yale-Princeton game, August 1907.

Set, orchestra, no. 2, 1A6.
  see: Orchestral set, no. 2.

S552 Set, orchestra, no. 2, 1C32.
    1911-1912 (?).
    Contents: (1) Largo: The Indians.—(2) Gup the blood or
    hearst.—(3) The last reader.
    x:
        (1) Largo: The Indians.
        (2) Gup the blood or hearst.
    sa:
        (1) The last reader.
        (2) The Indians.

Set, orchestra, no. 3, 1A8.
  see: Orchestral set, no. 3.

S553 Set, orchestra, no. 3, 1C35.
    1912–1918 (?).
    Contents: (1) Adagio sostenuto: At sea.—(2) Luck and
    work.—(3) Premonitions.
    Published:
        (1) Peer, 196(9?); first movement only.

x:

    (1) Adagio sostenuto, orchestra.

    (2) Pieces, basset horn, flute, percussion & 3 violins.

sa:

    (1) At sea.

    (2) Luck and work.

    (3) Premonitions.

S554 Set, orchestra, no. 4, 1C36.

    1906–1920 (?).

    Contents: (1) Andante cantabile: The last reader.—
      (2) Scherzo: The se'er.—(3) Largo to presto: The
      unanswered question.

    x:

      (1) Andante cantabile: The last reader.

      (2) Scherzo: The se'er.

      (3) Largo to presto: The unanswered question.

    sa:

      (1) The last reader.

      (2) The se'er.

      (3) The unanswered question.

S556 Set, orchestra, no. 5, 1C37.

    1908–1922 (?).

    Contents: (1) Like a sick eagle.—(2) Luck and work.—
      (3) Adagio: The Indians.

    x:

      (1) Adagio: The Indians.

    sa:

      (1) Like a sick eagle.

      (2) Luck and work.

      (3) The Indians.

S557 Set, orchestra, no. 6, 1C38.
ca. 1922 (?).
Notes: Never orchestrated (?).
Contents: (1) The new river.—(2) The Indians.—
(3) Ann Street.
x:
(1) Set, piano, saxophone & trumpet.
sa:
(1) The new river.
(2) The Indians.
(3) Ann Street.

Set, piano, saxophone & trumpet.
see: Set, orchestra, no. 6, 1C38.

S56 Set for theatre or chamber orchestra.
1906–1911; 1C28.
Alternate title: Theatre orchestra set.
Duration: 7'27".
Contents: (1) In the cage.—(2) In the inn.—(3) In the night.
Published:
(1) New Music, 1932 (Orchestra series, 5 no. 2);
reprinted by Presser, 1948; rental; AC37-2663rev*.
Recorded:
(1) Oceanic OCS-31; under title Three pieces for
piano & orchestra.
(2) Folkways FM-3348; contains In the inn, only.
(3) NMQR-1013; contains In the night, only.
(4) Vanguard VCS–10013.
x:
(1) Theatre orchestra set.
(2) Pieces, piano & orchestra.
(3) In the cage.

(4) In the inn.

(5) In the night.

sa:

(1) The cage.

S57 Set of cartoons or take-offs.

Orchestra.

1898-1907; 1C29.

Contents: (1) Rube trying to walk to 2 or 3, or All the way around and back.—(2) Mike Dolin—Johnny Evers, or Giants vs. Cubs.—(3) Willy Keeler.

x:

(1) Rube trying to walk to 2 or 3.

(2) Mike Dolin—Johnny Evers.

(3) Giants vs. Cubs.

(4) Cartoons or take-offs.

(5) Willy Keeler.

sa:

(1) All the way around and back.

S58 Set of overtures.

Orchestra.

1896–1898 (?); 1C11.

Alternate title: In these United States.

Notes: Lost; contents undetermined.

x:

(1) In these United States.

S59 Set of ragtime pieces, orchestra, 1C16.

1902.

Notes: Lost (contained nine items).

S591 Set of ragtime pieces, orchestra, 1C17.

1902–1904.

Notes: Score mostly lost (contained four items).

Set of three short pieces.
see: Set, bass & piano quintet.

S592 1776 [Seventeen seventy-six].
Orchestra.
1914–1915; 1B9.
Notes: Lost.
sa:
      (1) Overture and march "1776," orchestra.

A shadow made—a silhouette.
see: Largo risoluto, piano quintet, no. 2.

Shall we gather at the river . . .
see: At the river.

S61 She is not fair to outward view . . .
Voice & piano (Hartley Coleridge).
1894 (?); 6B18d.

S62 The side show.
Voice & piano (Charles E. Ives, after Pat Rooney).
1921; 6B66.
Published:
      (1) 6AA no. 32.
      (2) 6AG no. 10.
Recorded:
      (1) Concert Hall CHC-7.
      (2) Folkways FM-3344/5.
      (3) Nonesuch H-71209st.
x:
      (1) Is that Mr. Reilly . . .

The skies seemed true . . .
see: In autumn.

Skit for Danbury fair.
see: Danbury fair skit.

S63 Slants, or Christian & pagan.
    Men's voices & orchestra (in no. 1), chorus & organ
        (in no. 2); (Manlius, or Manilius).
    ca. 1911-1913; 5B7.
    Contents: (1) Duty.—(2) Vita.
    x:
        (1) Christian and pagan.
        (2) So nigh is grandeur . . .
        (3) Nascentes morimur . . .
        (4) Two slants.
        (5) Duty.
        (6) Vita.

S64 Slants, or Christian and pagan, voice & piano.
    (Ralph Waldo Emerson; Manlius, or Manilius).
    1921; 6B64a.
    Contents: (1) Duty.—(2) Vita.
    Published:
        (1) 6AA no. 9.
        (2) 6AA bis.
        (3) 6AC no. 1.
        (4) 6AE no. 1.
    Recorded:
        (1) Concert Hall CHC-7; contains Duty, only.

S65 Slow march, voice & piano.
    Medium voice & piano (Charles E. Ives).
    1888 (?); 6B10.
    Published:
        (1) 6AA no. 114.
        (2) 6AF no. 1.
    x:
        (1) One evening just at sunset . . .

S66 Slow march on Adeste fideles, band.
1886 or 1887 (?); 1D2.
Notes: Lost.
sa:
    (1) Adeste fideles in an organ prelude.

S67 Slugging a vampire.
Voice & piano (Charles E. Ives).
1902; 6B40c.
Notes: Revised version of Tarrant moss.
Published:
    (1) 6AD no. 10.
x:
    (1) I closed and drew . . .

S68 Sneak thief.
Chorus & orchestra (Charles E. Ives).
1914; 5B9a.
x:
    (1) People of the world . . .

So like a flower . . .
see: To Edith.

So long Harris . . .
see: Runaway horse on Main Street, voice & piano.

So may it be . . .
see: The rainbow.

So nigh is grandeur . . .
see: Slants, or Christian and pagan.

S69 Soliloquy.
Voice & piano, 4 hands (?); (Charles E. Ives).
1907; 6B43a.
Alternate title: A study in 7th and other things.

Published:
>   (1) 6AC no. 24.
Recorded:
>   (1) Nonesuch H-71209st.
x:
>   (1) When a man is sitting . . .

S71 Some southpaw pitching.
Piano.
1908; 3B17/21.
Notes: No. 21 of Studies, piano.
Published:
>   (1) Mercury, 1949; pl. no. 190.
Recorded:
>   (1) Folkways FM-3348.
x:
>   (1) Studies, piano.

Some things are undivined . . .
see: At sea.

S72 A son of a gambolier.
Voice & piano (traditional, Irish [?]).
1895; 6B22.
Published:
>   (1) 6AA no. 54.
>   (2) 6AJ no. 1.
x:
>   (1) Come join my humble ditty . . .

S73 A son of a gambolier; arr., band.
Notes: Arranged by Jonathan Elkus.
Published:
>   (1) Peer, 1962; 62-477951/M.
Recorded:
>   (1) Lehigh 1134.

112

S732 Sonata, organ, 3D16.
  1897 (?).
  Notes: Destroyed (?).

  Sonata, piano (three-page).
  see: Three-page sonata, piano.

S741 Sonata, piano, no. 1.
  1902–1910; 3A1.
  Contents: (1) Adagió con moto; andante con moto;
    allegro risoluto; adagio cantabile.—(2) Allegro moderato.
    —(3) Largo or adagio; allegro; largo.—(4) Andante;
    allegro; presto.—(5) Andante maestoso; adagio cantabile;
    allegro moderato ma con brio.
  Published:
      (1) Peer, 1954; pl. no. 258; introduction by
        Lou Harrison; M54-2325.
  Recorded:
      (1) Columbia MM-749; ML-4250; contains a
        movement entitled In the inn, only.
      (2) Columbia 72535/90.
      (3) Odyssey 32-16-0059.
      (4) RCA Victor LM-2941; LSC-2941st.
      (5) Desto 6458/61st.
      (6) Columbia ML-4490.
      (7) Nonesuch 1169; H-71169st.
      (8) Folkways FM-3348.
  x:
      (1) In the inn.

S742 Sonata, piano, no. 2.
  1909–1915 (essay completed in 1919); 3A2.
  Alternate title: Concord sonata.
  Contents: (1) Emerson.—(2) Hawthorne.—(3) The Alcotts.
    —(4) Thoreau.

Published:
  (1) Knickerbocker Press, 1920; contains essays, only.
  (2) Arrow (Associated Music Publishers), 1947;
      edited by John Kirkpatrick; M58-654.
  (3) Yale University, 1956; reproduction of Epilogue
      from essays; 68-42528/MN.
  (4) Dover, 1962; reprint of Knickerbocker Press
      edition of essays, only.
Recorded:
  (1) Columbia 72535/9D.
  (2) Columbia MM-749; ML 4250.
  (3) Composers Recordings Inc. CRI-150.
  (4) Time 58005; S-8005st.
  (5) Columbia MS-7192st.
  (6) Desto 6458/61st.
x:
  (1) Concord sonata.

S743 Sonata, piano, no. 3.
    1926–1927; 3A3.
    Notes: Unfinished; lost or destroyed.

S746 Sonata, trumpet & organ.
    1900; 2B7.
    Notes: Lost.

S747 Sonata, violin & piano, pre-pre-no. 1.
    1895 (?); 2C1.
    Notes: Consists of one movement-sketch (Prelude),
      remainder lost or destroyed.

S748 Sonata, violin & piano, pre-no. 1.
    1899–1903; 2C2.
    Notes: For publication of one version of the slow movement,
      see L32.

Contents: (1) Allegro moderato.—(2) Largo [2 versions].—
(3) Scherzo [rejected].—(4) Adagio; allegro.

S751 Sonata, violin & piano, no. 1.
1903–1909; 2C4.
Duration: 20'39".
Contents: (1) Andante; allegro vivace.—(2) Largo cantabile.
—(3) Allegro; andante cantabile; allegro primo.
Published:
(1) Peer, 1953; M54-1538.
Recorded:
(1) Lyrichord LL-17.
(2) Folkways FM-3346/7.
(3) Mercury MG-50096.
(4) Philips WSM-2-002; PHC-2-002st.

S752 Sonata, violin & piano, no. 2.
1903–1910; 2C5.
Duration: 14'11".
Contents: (1) Autumn: Adagio maestoso; andante con brio.
—(2) In the barn: Presto.—(3) The revival: Largo.
Published:
(1) G. Schirmer, 1951; pl. no. 42051.
Recorded:
(1) Polymusic PRLP-1001.
(2) Alco AR-101/2; contains 2d & 3d movements only.
(3) Columbia ML-2169; MM-987.
(4) Folkways FM-3346/7.
(5) Mercury MG-50096.
(6) Philips WSM-2-002; PHC-2-002st.
x:
(1) Autumn, violin & piano.
(2) In the barn.
(3) The revival.

S753 Sonata, violin & piano, no. 3.
   1902–1914; 2C6.
   Duration: 25'29".
   Contents: (1) Adagio.—(2) Allegro.—(3) Adagio
      (cantabile).
   Published:
         (1) New Music (Merion; Presser), 1951; pl. no.
            144-40019; v.34, no. 2, edited by Sol Babitz
            and Ingolf Dahl.
   Recorded:
         (1) Lyrichord LL-17.
         (2) Folkways FM-3346/7.
         (3) Mercury MG-50097.
         (4) Philips WSM-2-002; PHC-2-002st.

S754 Sonata, violin & piano, no. 4.
   1906 (?); 2C3.
   Alternate title: Children's day at the camp meeting.
   Duration: 9'29".
   Contents: (1) Allegro in a rather fast march time.—
      (2) Largo; allegro con slugarocko (faster and with
      action); andante; adagio; largo.—(3) Allegro.—
      (4) Adagio [rejected].
   Published:
         (1) Ives, 1915 (?).
         (2) Arrow (Associated Music Publishers), 1942.
   Recorded:
         (1) NMQR-1612.
         (2) Mercury MG-50442; 90442st.
         (3) Folkways FM-3346/7.
         (4) Mercury MG-50097.
         (5) Philips WSM-2-002; PHC-2-002st.
   x:
         (1) Children's day at the camp meeting.

S755 Sonata, violin & piano, no. 5.
    ca. 1915 (?); 2C7.
    Alternate title: New England holidays.
    Notes: Lost.
    x:
        (1) New England holidays.

S761 Song, 6B10b.
    1888.
    Notes: Title & words unknown.

S762 Song, 6B13a, G major.
    1891 (?).
    Notes: Title & words unknown.

S763 Song, 6B14b.
    1892.
    Notes: Title & words unknown.

S764 Song, 6B23a.
    1896 (?).
    Notes: Lost (?); title & words unknown.

S765 Song, 6B38a, E flat major.
    1901 (?).
    Notes: Music complete; title & words unknown.

S766 Song, 6B34c.
    1899.
    Notes: Unfinished (?); "words in 'Pike County' style."
    [Kirkpatrick].

S767 Song, 6B41b.
    1903.
    Notes: Lost; title & words unknown.

S768 Song—a poem of Kipling?

1908 (?); 6B29d.

Notes: Title from Kirkpatrick; title & words unknown.

Published:

(1) 6Aa no. 1.

(2) 6Ab no. 2.

S769 Song for a harvest season.

Voice & instrumental trio or organ (Greville Phillimore).

1893; 6B18.

Published:

(1) 6AC no. 32.

Recorded:

(1) Overtone LP-7.

(2) Nonesuch H-71222st.

x:

(1) Summer ended . . .

S771 A song—for anything.

Voice & piano (Charles E. Ives).

1898; 6B29e.

Published:

(1) 6AA no. 89.

(2) 6AH no. 1.

x:

(1) Yale farewell! . . .

S772 A song of Mory's.

TTBB (Charles Edmund Merrill, Jr.).

1897 (?); 5D10.

Published:

(1) Yale Courant, 1897, v.33, no.9, p.280-281.

x:

(1) When Flint stood without a peer . . .

S773 Songbook B.
    1898–1910 (?); 6Ab.
    Notes: For contents of these song copies and sketches,
    see Kirkpatrick, p. 148-149.

S774 Songbook C.
    1903 (?); 6Ac.
    Notes: For contents of these copies and sketches, see
    Kirkpatrick, p. 150.

S78 Songs, 6AA.
    Alternate title: 114 songs.
    Contents: (1) The majority.—(2) Evening.—(3) The last
    reader.—(4) At sea.—(5) Immortality.—(6) The
    new river.—(7) Disclosure.—(8) The rainbow.—
    (9) Two slants.—(10) Charlie Rutlage.—(11) Lincoln.—
    (12) Remembrance.—(13) Resolution.—(14) The Indians.
    —(15) The Housatonic at Stockbridge.—(16) Religion.—
    (17) Grantchester.—(18) Incantation.—(19) The
    greatest man.—(20) Hymn.—(21) Luck and work.—
    (22) An election.—(23) Maple leaves.—(24)
    Premonitions.—(25) Ann Street.—(26) Like a sick eagle.
    —(27) The swimmers.—(28) On the counter.—(29) The
    se'er.—(30) Paracelsus.—(31) Walt Whitman.—(32) The
    side show.—(33) Cradle song.—(34) La fède.—(35)
    August.—(36) September.—(37) December.—(38) The
    collection.—(39) Afterglow.—(40) The innate.—
    (41) 1, 2, 3.—(42) Serenity.—(43) The things our
    father loved.—(44) Watchman.—(45) At the river.—
    (46) His exaltation.—(47) The camp meeting.—
    (48) Thoreau.—(49) In Flanders field.—(50) He is there.
    —(51) Tom sails away.—(52) Old home day.—
    (53) In the alley.—(54) A son of a gambolier.—(55)
    Down east.—(56) The circus band.—(57) Mists [2d

setting].—(58) Evidence.—(59) Tolerance.—(60)
Autumn [2d setting].—(61) Nature's way.—(62) The
waiting soul.—(63) Those evening bells.—(64) The cage.
—(65) Spring song.—(66) The light that is felt.—
(67) Walking.—(68) Ilmenau.—(69) Rough wind.—
(70) Mirage.—(71) There is a lane.—(72) Tarrant moss.
—(73) Harpalus.—(74) The children's hour.—(75)
I travelled.—(76) Qu'il m'irait bien.—(77) Elégie.—
(78) Chanson de Florian.—(79) Rosamunde.—(80) Weil'
auf mir.—(81) The old mother.—(82) In summer fields.—
(83) Ich grolle nicht.—(84) Night of frost.—(85)
Dreams.—(86) Omens and oracles.—(87) An old flame.—
(88) A night song.—(89) A song—for anything.—
(90) The world's highway.—(91) Karen.—(92) Marie.—
(93) Berceuse.—(94) Where the eagle.—(95) Allegro.—
(96) Romanzo di Central Park.—(97) The south wind.—
(98) Naught that country needeth.—(99) Forward into
light.—(100) A Christmas carol.—(101) My native
land.—(102) Memories.—(103) The white gulls.—(104)
Two little flowers.—(105) West London.—(106)
Amphion).—(107) A night thought.—(108) Songs my
mother taught me.—(109) Waltz.—(110) The world's
wanderers.—(111) Canon: Oh, the days are gone.—
(112) To Edith.—(113) When stars).—(114) Slow march.
Published:
    (1) Ives (by G. Schirmer), 1921 [1922]; reprinted
      ca. 1925.
x:
    (1) Songs, 114.
sa: titles of contents.

S781 Songs, 6AA bis.
    Alternate title: 50 songs.

Contents: (1) Evening.—(2) The last reader.—(3) At sea.—
(4) Immortality.—(5) The new river.—(6) Disclosure.—
(7) Two slants.—(8) Charlie Rutlage.—(9) Remembrance.
—(10) Resolution.—(11) The Indians.—(12) Religion.—
(13) Grantchester.—(14) The greatest man.—(15)
Hymn.—(16) Like a sick eagle.—(17) Paracelsus.—
(18) Walt Whitman.—(19) Cradle song.—(20) La fède.—
(21) Watchman.—(22) Old home day.—(23) The circus
band.—(24) Mists [2d setting].—(25) Nature's way.—
(26) The waiting soul.—(27) Spring song:—(28) The
light that is felt.—(29) Walking.—(30) Ilmenau.—(31)
Mirage.—(32) There is a lane.—(33) The children's
hour.—(34) I travelled.—(35) Elégie.—(36) In summer
fields.—(37) Night of frost.—(38) Kären.—(39) Marie.—
(40) Berceuse.—(41) The south wind.—(42) Naught
that country needeth.—(43) A Christmas carol.—(44)
The white gulls.—(45) Two little flowers.—(46) West
London.—(47) Amphion.—(48) A night thought.—(49)
Songs my mother taught me.—(50) The world's
wanderers.—(51) To Edith.—(52) When stars [this
total of 52 titles taken from Kirkpatrick, p. 151-153,
indicating that the collection of 50 Songs actually contains
one more than the 51 normally stated].
Published:
(1) Redding, Conn., Ives, 1923; M59-448.
x:
(1) Songs, 50 [52].
sa: titles of contents.

S782 Songs, 6AB.
Alternate title: 7 songs.
Contents: (1) Evening.—(2) Charlie Rutlage.—(3) The
Indians.—(4) Maple leaves.—(5) The se'er.—(6)
Serenity.—(7) Walking.

Published:

> (1) Cos Cob (Arrow Press; Associated Music
> Publishers), 1932; pl. no. AMP 6621-16.

x:

> (1) Songs, 7.

sa: titles of contents.

S783 Songs, 6AC.

Alternate title: 34 songs.

Contents: (1) Two slants.—(2) Ann Street.—(3) At sea.—
(4) Walt Whitman.—(5) Immortality.—(6) The white
gulls.—(7) The greatest man.—(8) From the
"Incantations."—(9) September.—(10) Afterglow.—
(11) Premonitions.—(12) Luck and work.—(13) At the
river.—(14) From "The swimmers."—(15) Thoreau.—
(16) The rainbow.—(17) West London.—(18) December.
—(19) The new river.—(20) The last reader.—(21)
Mists.—(22) Like a sick eagle.—(23) Tolerance.—
(24) Soliloquy.—(25) Hymn.—(26) Harpalus.—(27)
Rough wind.—(28) The children's hour.—(29) The
south wind.—(30) Ich grolle nicht.—(31) A night
thought.—(32) Songs for the harvest season.—(33)
When stars are in the quiet skies.—(34) At parting.

Published:

> (1) New Music (Presser; Merion), 1933; pl. no.
> 441-41006; v.7, no. 1, Oct. 1933; AC37-2670rev3*.

x:

> (1) Songs, 34.

sa: titles of contents.

S784 Songs, 6AD.

Alternate title: 18 songs.

Contents: (1) General William Booth enters into heaven.—
(2) A farewell to land.—(3) Requiem.—(4) Cradle

122

song.—(5) La fède.—(6) Aeschylus and Sophocles.—
(7) Tom sails away.—(8) Canon: Oh, the days are gone.—
(9) The innate.—(10) Slugging a vampire.—(11) Two
little flowers.—(12) An election.—(13) From "Night
of frost in May."—(14) From "Paracelsus."—(15) A
Christmas carol.—(16) Majority.—(17) Resolution.—
(18) On the antipodes.—(19) In summer fields.
Published:
>   (1) New Music (Merion; Presser), 1935; pl. no.
>   441-41007; v.9, no.1, Oct. 1933; AC37-2678rev*.

x:
>   (1) Songs, 18 [19].

sa: titles of contents.

S785 Songs, 6Ad.
Alternate title: 2 songs.
Contents: (1) Tom sails away.—(2) The things our fathers
loved.
Published:
>   (1) Ives, 1917 or 1918; lithographed.

x:
>   (1) Songs, 2.

sa: titles of contents.

S786 Songs, 6AE.
Alternate title: 4 songs.
Contents: (1) Slants.—(2) 1, 2, 3.—(3) Luck and work
[Slants consists of Duty, and Vita].
Published:
>   (1) Mercury, 1933, 1950.

x:
>   (1) Songs, 4.

sa: titles of contents.

S787 Songs, 6Ae.

    Alternate title: 3 songs.

    Contents: (1) Afterglow.—(2) The innate.—(3) To Edith.

    Published:

        (1) Ives, ca. 1919; lithographed.

    x:

        (1) Songs, 3.

    sa: titles of contents.

S788 Songs, 6AF.

    Alternate title: 10 songs.

    Contents: (1) Slow march.—(2) To Edith.—(3) The circus
band.—(4) The world's wanderers.—(5) Amphion.—
(6) Memories.—(7) Forward into light.—(8) Omens and
oracles.—(9) I travelled among unknown men.—
(10) Mirage.

    Published:

        (1) Peer, 1953.

    x:

        (1) Songs, 10.

    sa: titles of contents.

S79 Songs, 6AG.

    Alternate title: 12 songs.

    Contents: (1) Kären.—(2) Waltz.—(3) My native land
[1st setting].—(4) Qu'il m'irait bien.—(5) Spring song.—
(6) The waiting soul.—(7) August.—(8) Religion.—
(9) Remembrance.—(10) The side show.—(11) The
Housatonic at Stockbridge.—(12) Disclosure.

    Published:

        (1) Peer, 1954; M56-1141.

    x:

        (1) Songs, 12.

    sa: titles of contents

S791 Songs, 6AH.
>   Alternate title: 14 songs.
>   Contents: (1) A song—for anything.—(2) Songs my mother
>   taught me.—(3) Marie.—(4) Rosamunde.—(5) Naught
>   that country needeth.—(6) Romanzo di Central Park.—
>   (7) Weil' auf mir.—(8) The cage.—(9) Those evening
>   bells.—(10) Nature's way.—(11) Watchman.—(12) The
>   things our fathers loved.—(13) In Flanders field.—
>   (14) On the counter.
>   Published:
>>   (1) Peer, 1955; M56-1699.
>   x:
>>   (1) Songs, 14.
>   sa: titles of contents.

S793 Songs, 6AJ.
>   Alternate title: 9 songs.
>   Contents: (1) A son of a gambolier.—(2) Dreams.—
>   (3) Elégie.—(4) There is a lane.—(5) Autumn.—
>   (6) Evidence.—(7) His exaltation.—(8) They are there.—
>   (9) Grantchester.
>   Published:
>>   (1) Peer, 1956; M57-1178.
>   x:
>>   (1) Songs, 9.
>   sa: titles of contents.

S794 Songs, 6AK.
>   Alternate title: 13 songs.
>   Contents: (1) Abide with me.—(2) The world's highway.—
>   (3) An old flame.—(4) In the alley.—(5) Where the
>   eagle.—(6) Allegro.—(7) Berceuse.—(8) The old mother.
>   —(9) Tarrant moss.—(10) The camp meeting.—

(11) Down east.—(12) The collection.—(13) Old home
day.
Published:
    (1) Peer, 1958; M58-1388.
x:
    (1) Songs, 13.
sa: titles of contents.

S795 Songs, 6AL.
    Alternate title: 3 songs.
    Contents: (1) The greatest man.—(2) Two little flowers.—
    (3) Where the eagle.
    Published:
        (1) Associated Music Publishers, 1969.
    x:
        (1) Songs, 3.
    sa: titles of contents.

Songs, 2.
  see: Songs, 6Ad.

Songs, 3.
  see: Songs, 6Ae.
    Songs, 6AL.

Songs, 4.
  see: Songs, 6AE.

Songs, 7.
  see: Songs, 6AB.

Songs, 9.
  see: Songs, 6AJ.

Songs, 10.
  see: Songs, 6AF.

126

Songs, 12.
see: Songs, 6AG.

Songs, 13.
see: Songs, 6AK.

Songs, 14.
see: Songs, 6AH.

Songs, 18 [19].
see: Songs, 6AD.

Songs, 34.
see: Songs, 6AC.

Songs, 50 [52].
see: Songs, 6AA bis.

Songs, 114.
see: Songs, 6AA.

Songs, Sacred.
see: Sacred songs.

Songs! Visions of my homeland . . .
see: Down east.

S81 Songs and harmonizations.
Alternate title (publisher's title): Eleven songs and two
harmonizations.
Contents: (1) Rock of ages.—(2) Far from my heav'nly
home.—(3) There is a certain garden.—(4) A Scotch
lullaby.—(5) God bless and keep thee.—(6) No more.—
(7) Pictures.—(8) The one way.—(9) Peaks.—(10) Yellow
leaves.—(11) A sea dirge.—(12) Christmas carol.—
(13) In the mornin'.
Published:
(1) Associated Music Publishers, 1968; edited by
John Kirkpatrick; 72-207273.
sa: titles of contents.

S82 Songs my mother taught me.
   Voice & piano (Adolf Heyduk; Natalie Macfarren, trans.).
   1895; 6B21c.
   Published:
         (1) 6AA no. 108.
         (2) 6AA bis.
         (3) 6AH no. 2.
   Songs of the First World War.
   see: In Flanders field.

A sound of a distant horn . . .
   see: In Flanders field.

S83 The south wind.
   Voice & piano (Harmony T. Ives).
   1907; 6B44.
   Published:
         (1) 6AA no. 97.
         (2) 6AA bis.
         (3) 6AC no. 29.
   x:
         (1) When gently blows the south wind . . .

Space and duration.
   see: The gong on the hook and ladder.

S84 Spring song.
   Voice & piano (Harmony T. Ives).
   1907; 6B43.
   Published:
         (1) 6AA no. 65.
         (2) 6AA bis.
         (3) 6AG no. 5.
         (4) 6Ab no. 8-9.
   x:
         (1) Across the hill of late . . .

S85 Stars of the summer night . . .
    SATB (Henry Wadsworth Longfellow).
    1891 (?); 5D2.

S92 Studies, piano.
    1907–1912 (?); 3B17.
    Contains 27 movements, of which nos. 1, 4, 10-19 and 23-26
        are lost or incomplete; no. 9 bears title, The
        anti-abolitionist riots; no. 21 bears title, Some
        southpaw pitching; no. 22 bears title, Twenty-two;
        no. 27 bears title, Chromâtimelôdtune.
    Recorded:
        (1) Desto 6458/61st; contains excerpts only.
    sa:
        (1) The anti-abolitionist riots.
        (2) Some southpaw pitching.
        (3) Twenty-two.
        (4) Chromâtimelôdtune.

A study in 7ths and other things.
    see: Soliloquy.

Summer ended . . .
    see: Song for a harvest season.

S95 The sun shines hot on quarry walls . . .
    Voice & piano.
    1897 (?); 6B25d.

S96 Sunrise.
    Voice & piano (Charles E. Ives).
    1926; 6B77.
    Notes: Unfinished (?).
    x:
        (1) A light low in the East . . .

Sunset and evening star . . .
   see: Crossing the bar.

The sweetest flow'r . . .
   see: At parting.

S97 The swimmers.
   Voice & piano (Louis Untermeyer).
   1915–1921; 6B53.
   Published:
      (1) 6AA no. 27.
      (2) 6AC no. 14.
   Recorded:
      (1) Overtone LP-7.
      (2) Folkways FM-3344/5.
      (3) Nonesuch H-71209st.
   x:
      (1) Then the swift plunge . . .
      (2) From "The swimmers."

S98 The swimmers, orchestra.
   1922 (?); 1C39.
   Notes: Projected orchestration.

A symphony: Holidays.
   see: Holidays.

Symphony, Universal.
   see: Universe symphony.

S991 Symphony, no. 1, D minor.
   1896–1898; 1A1.
   Contents: (1) Allegro moderato.—(2) Adagio molto;
     sostenuto.—(3) Scherzo; vivace.—(4) Allegro molto.
   Published:
      (1) Peer, 196–; rental.

Recorded:
> (1) Columbia MS-7111st.
> (2) Vanguard C-10032/4; VCS-10032/4st.
> (3) Columbia D-35783.
> (4) RCA Victor LM-2893; LSC-2893st.

S992 Symphony, no. 2.
> 1897–1909; 1A2.
> Contents: (1) Andante moderato.—(2) Allegro.—(3) Adagio cantabile.—(4) Lento maestoso.—(5) Allegro molto vivace.
> Published:
>> (1) Southern Music Publishing Co., 1951.
>
> Recorded:
>> (1) Society of Participating Artists SPA-39.
>> (2) Columbia KL-5489; KS-6155st.
>> (3) Vanguard C-10032/4; VCS-10032/4st.
>> (4) Columbia D3S-783.
>> (5) Columbia ML-6289.

S993 Symphony, no. 3.
> 1904–1911; 1A3.
> Alternate title: The camp meeting.
> Contents: (1) Andante (The camp meeting).—(2) Allegro (Children's day).—(3) Largo (Communion).
> Published:
>> (1) Arrow, 1947.
>> (2) Associated Music Publishers, 1964; pl. no. AMP–9623; 64-45652/M.
>
> Recorded:
>> (1) WCFM LP-1.
>> (2) Vanguard VRS-468.
>> (3) Mercury MG-50149; 90149st.
>> (4) RCA Victor LSC-3060st.

(5) Vanguard C-10032/4; VCS-10032/4st.
(6) Columbia D3S-783.
(7) Columbia ML-6243.

x:

(1) The camp meeting.
(2) Communion.
(3) Children's day.

S994 Symphony, no. 4.
1910–1916; 1A7.
Contents: (1) Prelude: Maestoso; adagio.—(2) Scherzo: Allegretto.—(3) Fugue in C minor: Andante con moto.—(4) Finale: Very slowly or adagio.
Published:
(1) New Music, 1929; v.2, no. 2, Jan. 1929; first and second movements only.
(2) Associated Music Publishers, 1965; pl. no. AMP-96537; edited by John Kirkpatrick; 66-53435/M.
Recorded:
(1) Columbia ML-6175; MS-6775st.
(2) Columbia D3S-783.
(3) Vanguard C-10032/4st.

S9942 Symphony, no. 4. Fugue; arr., orchestra.
Notes: Arranged by Bernard Hermann.

S9943 Symphony, no. 4. Fugue; arr., piano.
Notes: Arranged by John Kirkpatrick.

TSAIJ.
see: Trio, piano & strings.

T13 Take–offs.
Piano.
1906–1907 (?); 3B16.

Notes: Title from Kirkpatrick.
Contents: (1) The seen and unseen, or sweet and tough.—
(2) Rough and ready et al and/or The jumping frog.
—(3) Song without (good) words, or Melody in F
and F flat.—(4) Scene episode.—(5) Bad resolutions
and good wan [sic].
Recorded:
(1) Desto 6458/61st.

T19 Tarrant moss.
Voice & piano (Rudyard Kipling).
1902; 6B29c.
Notes: Revised as Slugging a vampire.
Published:
(1) 6AA no. 72.
(2) 6AK no. 9.
(3) 6Aa no. 2.
(4) 6Ab no. 3.
Recorded:
(1) Overtone LP-7.
x:
(1) Poems of Kipling.
sa:
(1) Slugging a vampire.

T25 Te Deum.
Chorus.
1888–1900 (?); 5C8.
Notes: Lost.
x:
(1) We praise thee, O God . . .

Tell me, star whose wings of light . . .
see: The world's wanderers.

A tender child of summers . . .
see: The light that is felt.

Thanksgiving Day.
see: Holidays.

That night on Judges' walk . . .
see: Judges' walk.

Theatre orchestra set.
see: Set for theatre or chamber orchestra.

T37 Thee I love.
Voice & piano (John Wesley, trans.).
1898 (?); 6B28c.

Then the swift plunge . . .
see: The swimmers.

There comes o'er the valley . . .
see: Evidence.

T41 There is a certain garden . . .
Voice & piano.
1893; 6B17.
Published:
(1) Songs and harmonizations.

T42 There is a lane.
Voice & piano (Harmony T. Ives).
1902; 6B39c.
Published:
(1) 6AA no. 71.
(2) 6AA bis.
(3) 6AJ no. 4.

T43 There is no unbelief.
     Chorus (James T. Bixby, after Lizzie York Case).
     1902; 5C40.
     Notes: Lost.
     sa:
          (1) Religion.

There was the lyre of earth . . .
     see: Night of frost in May.

There's a shadow on the grass . . .
     see: Premonitions.

There's a time in many a life . . .
     see: They are there!

T44 They are there!, chorus & orchestra.
     Unison voices & orchestra (Charles E. Ives).
     1942; 5B14.
     Published:
          (1) Peer, 1961; edited by Lou Harrison; 62-28990/M.
     x:
          (1) There's a time in many a life . . .

T45 They are there!, voice & piano.
     (Charles E. Ives).
     1942; 6B79.
     Alternate title: A war song march.
     Notes: Revision of He is there!
     Published:
          (1) 6AJ no. 8.
          (2) Peer, 196–.
     x:
          (1) There's a time in many a life . . .
          (2) A war song march.
     sa:
          (1) He is there! May 30, 1917.

They walked beside the summer sea . . .
see: No more.

T46 The things our fathers loved.
Voice & piano (Charles E. Ives).
1917; 6B58.
Alternate title: The greatest of these is liberty.
Published:
(1) 6AA no. 43.
(2) 6AH no. 12.
(3) 6Ad no. 2.
x:
(1) The greatest of these is liberty.
(2) I think there must be a place . . .

This is the day of light . . .
see: Let there be light.

This scherzo is a joke.
see: Trio, piano & strings.

T48 Thoreau.
Voice & piano (Charles E. Ives, after H. D. Thoreau).
1915; 6B52.
Published:
(1) 6AA no. 48.
(2) 6AC no. 15.
Recorded:
(1) Concert Hall CHC-7.
x:
(1) He grew in those seasons . . .

T52 Those evening bells.
Voice & piano (Thomas Moore).
1907; 6B42d.

Published:

    (1) 6AA no. 63.

    (2) 6AH no. 9.

Thou hidden love of God . . .
see: Hymn, 6B62.

Thoughts which deeply rest . . .
see: Disclosure.

T53 Three-page sonata, piano.
    1905; 3B15.
    Published:

        (1) Mercury, 1949; pl. no. 191.

    Recorded:

        (1) Folkways FM-3348.

        (2) Cambridge 804; 1804st.

        (3) Desto 6458/61st.

    x:

        (1) Sonata, piano (three-page).

T54 Three places in New England.
    1903–1914; 1A5.
    Alternate title: Three New England Places.—New England
      symphony.—Orchestral set, no. 1.
    Duration: 25′.
    Contents: (1) St. Gaudens in Boston Common.—(2)
      Putnam's camp.—(3) The Housatonic at Stockbridge.
    Published:

        (1) C. C. Birchard (Mercury; Presser), 1935.

    Recorded:

        (1) Artist JS-13; LP-100; 1404; contains The
           Housatonic, only.

        (2) American Recording Society ARS-27; ARS-116.

        (3) Mercury H-50149; MG-90149st.

(4) Desto 403; DST-6403st.

(5) Columbia ML-6084; MS-6684st.

(6) Everest 6118; contains The Housatonic, only.

(7) Columbia ML-6415.

(8) Columbia MS-7111.

(9) RCA Victor LM-2959; LSC-2959st.

x:

(1) A New England symphony.

(2) Orchestral set, no. 1.

(3) Boston Common.

(4) Putnam's camp.

(5) Set, orchestra, no. 1, 1A5.

(6) The St. Gaudens.

sa:

(1) The Housatonic at Stockbridge.

T55 Through night and day.
Voice & piano (Charles E. Ives, after John S. B. Monsell).
1896; 6B15a.

x:

(1) I dream of thee . . .

T62 To Edith.
Medium voice & piano (Harmony T. Ives).
1919; 6B60.
Published:

(1) 6AA no. 112.

(2) 6AA bis.

(3) 6AF no. 2.

(4) 6Ae no. 3.

x:

(1) So like a flower . . .

T63 To love someone more dearly . . .
Voice & piano (Maude Louise Ray).
1895 (?); 6B21e.

T64 Toccata, organ, 3D21.
1901,
Notes: Lost.

T65 Tolerance.
Voice & piano (Rudyard Kipling, quoted by Arthur T.
Hadley).
1909; 6B45e.
Published:
(1) 6AA no. 59.
(2) 6AC no. 23.
Recorded:
(1) Society of Participating Artists SPA-9.
x:
(1) How can I turn . . .

T66 Tom sails away.
Voice & piano (Charles E. Ives).
1917; 6B59.
Published:
(1) 6AA no. 51.
(2) 6AD no. 7.
(3) 6Ad no. 1.
Recorded:
(1) Overtone LP-7.
(2) Folkways FM-3344/5.
x:
(1) Scenes from my childhood . . .

T67 Tone roads, no. 1.
     Chamber orchestra.
     1911; 1C34/i.
     Notes: No. 1 of Tone roads et al.
     Published:
             (1) Peer, 1949; pl. no. 18-7.
     Recorded:
             (1) Cambridge 804; 1804st.
     x:
             (1) Tone roads et al.

T68 Tone roads, no. 2.
     Orchestra.
     1911–1919; 1C34/ii.
     Notes: No. 2 of Tone roads et al; lost (?).

T69 Tone roads, no. 3.
     Chamber orchestra.
     1915; 1C34/iii.
     Notes: No. 3 of Tone roads et al.
     Published:
             (1) Peer, 1952; M53-618.
     Recorded:
             (1) Cambridge 804; 1804st.

   Tone roads et al.
     see: Tone roads, no. 1.
        Tone roads, no. 2.
        Tone roads, no. 3.

T74 Town, gown and state overture.
     Band.
     1896; 1D7.
     Notes: Lost.
     x:
             (1) Overture: Town, gown and state.

T77 Transcriptions from Emerson.
Piano.
1917–1921 (?); 3B21.
Notes: Contains four movements.

T83 Trio, piano, clarinet & violin.
1902–1903; 2B9.
Notes: Lost; may be related to Largo for the same
instrumentation.
sa:
(1) Largo, piano, clarinet & violin.

T84 Trio, piano & strings.
Piano, violin & violoncello.
1904–1911; 2B17.
Contents: (1) Andante moderato.—(2) T[his] s[cherzo]
i[s] a j[oke]: Presto, più mosso; adagio; allegro moderato;
allegro assai; adagio; presto.—(3) Moderato con moto;
andante sostenuto; maestoso; andante con moto;
allegro.
Published:
(1) Peer, 1955.
Recorded:
(1) Decca DL-10126; DG-710. 162st.
x:
(1) TSIAJ.
(2) This scherzo is a joke.

Tunes we heard in ninety-two . . .
see: On the counter.

T95 Turn ye, turn ye.
SATB & piano or organ (Josiah Hopkins).
1889-1890; 5C11.

Published:

(1) Mercury (Presser), 1955.

Recorded:

(1) Society for the Preservation of the American Musical Heritage MTA-116.

x:

(1) O turn ye . . .

T96 Twenty-two.

Piano.

1912 (?); 3B117/22.

Notes: No. 22 of Studies for piano.

Published:

(1) New Music (Presser), 1947.

Recorded:

(1) Folkways FM-3348.

x:

(1) Studies, piano.

Two slants.

see: Slants, or Christian and pagan.

T97 Two little flowers.

Voice & piano (Charles E. Ives, and Harmony T. Ives).

1921; 6B68.

Published:

(1) 6AA no. 104.

(2) 6AA bis.

(3) 6AD no. 11.

(4) 6AL no. 2.

(5) Ives, ca. 1921.

Recorded:

(1) Concert Hall CHC-7.

(2) NMQR–1412.

> (3) Overtone LP-7.
> (4) Folkways FM-3344/5.

x:

> (1) Oh sunny days . . .

Über allen Gipfeln ist Rüh . . .
see: Ilmenau: Over all the treetops.

U54 The unanswered question.
Orchestra.
1906; 1C25.
Alternate title: A cosmic landscape.—(no. 1 of) Two
contemplations.
Duration: 5'02".
Published:

> (1) Boletín Latino-Americano de Música, 1941;
> v.5, no.5, October 1941, p.156-162, published
> under title La pregunta incontestada.
> (2) Southern Music Publishing Co., 1953; pl. no.
> 246-5; M54-2151.

Recorded:

> (1) Polymusic PRLP-1001; issued as Pieces for
> orchestra.
> (2) Siena S-100-2st.
> (3) Unicorn UNLP-1037.
> (4) Vanguard VCS-10013st.
> (5) Columbia ML-6243.
> (6) RCA Victor LM-2893; LSC-2893st.
> (7) Turnabout TV-34154.

x:

> (1) A cosmic landscape.
> (2) La pregunta incontestada.
> (3) Pieces for orchestra.
> (4) Contemplations.

sa:
>   (1) Set, orchestra, no. 4, 1C36.

Under the wide and starry sky . . .
see: Requiem.

Universal symphony.
see: Universe symphony.

U58 Universe symphony.
1911–1928; 1A9.
Alternate title: Universal symphony.
Notes: Unfinished; contains 3 sections.
x:
>   (1) Universal symphony.
>   (2) Symphony, Universal.

Unto thee, O God . . .
see: Psalm 25.

Variations on a national hymn.
see: Variations on America, organ.

V31 Variation on America, organ.
1891 or 1892 (?); 4D5.
Published:
>   (1) Music Press, 1949; (Music Press organ series
>   MP-601); published with Adeste fideles in an
>   organ prelude; 50-28932rev2/M.

Recorded:
>   (1) Columbia ML-5496; MS-6161st.
>   (2) Nonesuch H-71200st.

x:
>   (1) America.
>   (2) Variations on a national hymn.

sa:
>   (1) Adeste fideles in an organ prelude.

V32 Variations on America, organ; arr., band.
    Duration: about 7 minutes.
    Notes: Arranged by William Schuman.
    Published:
        (1) Merion Music (Presser), 1968 (Presser summit
            band series); 70-207283.

V33 Variations on America, organ; arr., orchestra.
    Duration: 8'.
    Notes: Arranged by William Schuman.
    Published:
        (1) Merion Music (Presser), 1964; pl. no. 446-41010;
            65-39127/M.
    Recorded:
        (1) LOU-651.
        (2) RCA Victor LM-2893; LSC-2893st.

V34 Variations on Jerusalem the golden, organ.
    1888–1889 (?); 3D3.
    x:
        (1) Jerusalem the golden.

Varied air and variations, piano.
    see: Protests.

V57 Vesper service.
    Chorus.
    1893–1894 (?); 5C23.
    Notes: Lost.

Vita.
    see: Slants, or Christian and pagan.

Der voll Mond . . .
    see: Rosamunde.

Voices live in every finite being . . .
    see: The innate.

145

V94 Voluntary, organ, 3D1, C minor.
     1887 (?).
     Notes: Unfinished or lost (?); title from Kirkpatrick.

V95 Voluntary, organ, 3D2, F major.
     1887 (?).
     Notes: Unfinished or lost (?); title from Kirkpatrick.

V97 Vote for names.
     Voice (or voices) & (3) piano(s); (Charles E. Ives).
     1912; 6B48a.
     Published:
          (1) Peer, 1968; pl. 2014-2; version for voice & piano.
          (2) Peer, 1968; pl. 2014-3; version for voice(s) &
              piano(s); 68-129356/M.
     x:
          (1) After trying hard to think . . .

W14 The waiting soul.
     Low voice & piano (William Cowper).
     1908; 6B44a.
     Published:
          (1) 6AA no. 62.
          (2) 6AA bis.
          (3) 6AG no. 6.
          (4) Sacred songs.
     x:
          (1) Breathe from the gentle South . . .
     Wake! Wake, earth . . .
     see: Easter carol.

W17 Walking.
     Voice & piano (Charles E. Ives).
     1902; 6B40.

Published:
- (1) 6AA no. 67.
- (2) 6AA bis.
- (3) Arrow (Associated Music Publishers), 1939.
- (4) 6AB no. 7.

Recorded:
- (1) Overtone LP-7.
- (2) Educo 4006.
- (3) Folkways 3344/5.

x:
- (1) A big October morning . . .

Walking stronger under distant skies . . .
see: Resolution.

W23 Walt Whitman.
Chorus (Walt Whitman).
1913; 5B8.
x:
- (1) Who goes there . . .

W24 Walt Whitman, voice & piano.
(Walt Whitman).
1921; 6B64c.
Published:
- (1) 6AA no. 31.
- (2) 6AA bis.
- (3) 6AC no. 4.

Recorded:
- (1) Society of Participating Artists SPA-9.

x:
- (1) Who goes there . . .

W25 Waltz, voice & piano.
(Charles E. Ives).
1893-1895 (?); 6B19.

Published:
>   (1) 6AA no. 109.
>   (2) 6AG no. 2.

x:
>   (1) Round and round the old dance ground . . .

W26 Waltz-rondo, piano.
>   1911; 3B18.

A war song march.
>   see: They are there!

Washington's Birthday.
>   see: Holidays.

W31 Watchman.
>   Soprano & organ (John Bowring).
>   1901; 6B39.
>   Notes: Lost.

sa:
>   (1) Piece on Watchman, orchestra.

W32 Watchman, voice & piano.
>   (John Bowring).
>   1913; 6B48d.
>   Published:
>   (1) 6AA no. 44.
>   (2) 6AA bis.
>   (3) 6AH no. 11.
>   (4) Sacred songs.

sa:
>   (1) Piece on Watchman, orchestra.

We also have our pest . . .
>   see: Aeschylus and Sophocles.

We in this world today . . .
    see: Grace.

We praise thee, O God . . .
    see: Te Deum.

W42 Weil' auf mir.
    Voice & piano (Nikolaus Lenau; Elisabeth Rücker &
        Westbrook [Charles E. Ives?], trans.).
    1902; 6B39b.
    Published:
        (1) 6AA no. 80.
        (2) 6AH no. 7.
    x:
        (1) Eyes so dark . . .

We're sitting in the opera house . . .
    see: Memories.

W52 West London.
    Voice & piano (Matthew Arnold).
    1921; 6B64.
    Published:
        (1) 6AA no. 105.
        (2) 6AA bis.
        (3) 6AC no. 17.
    Recorded:
        (1) Folkways 3344/5.
        (2) Nonesuch H-71209st.
    x:
        (1) Crouch'd on the pavement . . .

What have you done for me . . .
    see: Because of you.

What we want is honest money . . .
    see: William Will.

When a man is sitting . . .
see: Soliloquy.

When fell the gloom . . .
see: Johnny Poe.

When Flint stood without a peer . . .
see: A song of Mory's.

When gently blows the south wind . . .
see: The south wind.

W56 When spring grows old . . .
Voice & piano (Maurice Thompson).
1899 (?); 6B34b.

W57 When stars are in the quiet skies.
Voice & piano (Bulwer-Lytton).
1891-1892 (?); 6B13.
Published:
    (1) 6AA no. 113.
    (2) 6AA bis.
    (3) 6AC no. 33.
Recorded:
    (1) Society of Participating Artists SPA-9.

When the distant evening bell . . .
see: Nature's way.

W58 When the moon is on the wave.
Instrumental septet & voice (Lord Byron).
ca. 1908; 1C31/vi.
Notes: No. 6 of Set, orchestra, no. 1, 1C31.
Published:
    (1) Peer, 1958.
x:
    (1) Set, orchestra, no. 1, 1C31.

(2) Byron's When the moon is on the wave.

(3) Allegretto sombreoso.

sa:

(1) Incantation.

W59 When the waves softly sigh . . .
Voice & piano.
1892; 6B14.
Published:
(1) 6AA no. 89.
(2) 6AH no. 1.

When twilight comes . . .
see: Dreams.

Where dreams enfold me . . .
see: An old flame.

W61 Where the eagle.
Medium voice & piano (Monica Peveril Turnbull).
1900; 6B42b.
Published:
(1) 6AA no. 94.
(2) 6AK no. 5.
(3) 6AL no. 3.
(4) Cos Cob Song Book (Arrow, Boosey & Hawkes).
(5) Sacred Songs.
Recorded:
(1) Overtone LP-7.

While one will search . . .
see: Luck and work.

W62 The white gulls.
Voice & piano (Russian text; Maurice Morris, trans.).
1921; 6B67c.

Published:
> (1) 6AA no. 103.
> (2) 6AA bis.
> (3) 6AC no. 6.

Recorded:
> (1) Overtone LP-7.
> (2) Folkways FM-3344/5.

Who dares to say . . .
see: Immortality.

Who goes there . . .
see: Walt Whitman.

W63 Who knows the light . . .
Voice & piano.
1900 (?); 6B35a.

Why doesn't one, two, three . . .
see: One, two, three.

W64 Wie Melodien zieht es mir.
Voice & piano (Klaus Groth).
1898 (?); 6B29a.

W65 Wiegenlied.
Voice & piano (German folk text).
1900 (?); 6B36a.
Published:
> (1) 6Ac no. 27 (?).

x:
> (1) Guten Abend . . .

W71 William Will.
Voice & piano (Susan Benedict Hill?).
1896; 6B24.

Notes: Song for McKinley campaign.
Published:
> (1) Willis Woodward & Co., 1896.

x:
> (1) What we want is honest money . . .

Willy Keeler.
see: Set of cartoons or take-offs.

W84 Wohl wanchen Rosenzweig . . .
Voice & piano (Karl Stieler).
1900 (?); 6B35b.

W92 The world's highway.
Voice & piano (Harmony T. Ives).
1896 or 1897; 6B42c.
Published:
> (1) 6AA no. 90.
> (2) 6AK no. 2.

x:
> (1) For long I wander'd happily . . .

W93 The world's wanderers.
Medium voice & piano (Percy B. Shelley).
1895; 6B22d.
Published:
> (1) 6AA no. 110.
> (2) 6AA bis.
> (3) 6AF no. 4.

x:
> (1) Tell me, star whose wings of light . . .

Would I were in Grantchester . . .
see: Grantchester.

Yale farewell! . . .
see: A song—for anything.

Y16 Yale-Princeton football game.
     Orchestra.
     1899; 1B3.
     Notes: Lost.
     sa:
          (1) Yale-Princeton game, August 1907.

Y17 Yale-Princeton game, August 1907.
     Orchestra.
     1908; 1C31/6a.
     Notes: No. 6 1/2 of Set, orchestra, no. 1, 1C31.
     x:
          (1) Set, orchestra, no. 1, 1C31.
     sa:
          (1) Yale-Princeton football game.

Y39 The year's at spring.
     SATB (Robert Browning).
     1888 or 1889 (?); 5D1.

Y43 Yellow leaves.
     Voice & piano (Henry Bellamann).
     1923 (?); 6B73.
     Published:
          (1) Songs and harmonizations.
     x:
          (1) Heart-shaped yellow leaves . . .

   The young May moon . . .
     see: A night song.

Publication Index

Care has been taken to cite the titles under the name of the current publisher, not without a register of those previously engaged in the printing of the edition in question. This index does not include titles within anthologies; each indication is for a single publication.

Arrow Press.
    see: Associated Music Publishers, Inc.
    Boosey & Hawkes.

Associated Music Publishers, Inc., 609 Fifth Avenue, New York, N. Y., 10036. Works originally issued with Arrow imprint are now reprinted unchanged by Associated Music Publishers.

C41 Central Park in the dark.
    Bomart, 1949 (Outdoor scenes). Rental.

G78 The greatest man.
    Arrow, 1939. Replaced by S795.

H19 Hallowe'en.
    Bomart, 1949 (Outdoor scenes). Version piano quintet on sale; version for string orchestra on rent.

H75 Holidays.
    Washington's Birthday: New Music Editions, 1936
        (Orchestra series, no. 20). Rental.
    The Fourth of July: New Music Editions, 1932
        (Orchestra series, no. 3). Rental.

P79 The pond.
  Bomart, 1949 (Outdoor scenes). Rental.

P976 Psalm 67.
  Arrow, 1939 (AMP no. A274).

S52 Serenity, unison voice(s) & piano.
  Arrow, 1939. Out of print.
  Associated Music Publishers, 1942 (AMP
    no. 96233-2; A-377).

S742 Sonata, piano, no. 2.
  Arrow, 1947 (John Kirkpatrick, ed.).

S754 Sonata, violin & piano, no. 4.
  Arrow, 1942.

S782 Songs, 6AB (Seven songs).
  Cos Cob, 1932; reprinted by Arrow, 1939; reprinted by
    Associated Music Publishers. (AMP no. 6621-16).

S795 Songs, 6AL (Three songs).
  Associated Music Publishers, 1969.

S81 Songs and harmonizations.
  Associated Music Publishers, 1969 (John Kirkpatrick, ed.).

S993 Symphony, no. 3.
  Arrow, 1947. Out of print.
  Associated Music Publishers, 1964 (AMP no. 9623).
  Performance materials on rent.

S994 Symphony, no. 4.
  1st & 2d movements: New Music Editions, 1929 (II-2).
    Out of print.
  Associated Music Publishers, 1965 (AMP no. 96537).
  Performance materials on rent.

Y44 Yellow leaves.
  Associated Music Publishers, 19??. Replaced by S81.

Birchard, C. C.
  see: Presser.

Boletín Latino-Americano de Música. Montevideo: Instituto Interamericano
  de Musicología, Paña & Cie., v.5, no.5, October 1941, p.56–162.
  U54 The unanswered question (La pregunta incontestada).

Bomart, Hillsdale, N. Y.
  see: Associated Music Publishers, Inc.

Boosey & Hawkes, Oceanside, N. Y., 11592.

    W61 Where the eagle.
        Cos Cob, 1963; Arrow, 19——; Boosey & Hawkes (Cos Cob Song
        Book). Copyright owned by Associated Music Publishers.

Columbia Broadcasting System Music Library, New York, N. Y.

    I612 Intercollegiate march, band; arr., orchestra.
        Arranged by Bernard Hermann. Not available for sale or rent.

Cos Cob.
    see: Associated Music Publishers, Inc.
    Boosey & Hawkes.

Fischer (Carl) Inc., 62 Cooper Square, New York, N. Y., 10003.

    T54 Three places in New England.
        Carl Fischer, 19——. Out of print.

Ives (Charles Edward).
    Works privately published by Ives, never available commercially,
    are not listed in this index.

MJQ Music Inc., 200 West 57 Street, New York, N. Y., 10019.

    C61 Chromâtimelôdtune; arr., chamber orchestra.
        MJQ Music, 1963, 1967 (MJQ no. 16). Reconstructed and
        completed by Gunther Schuller. Parts on rent.

Mercury Music Corporation, 17 West 60 Street, New York, N. Y., 10023.

    A41b The all-enduring, voice & piano.
        Mercury (under contract for publication in 1969).

Merion Music, Inc.
    see: Presser.

Molineux (George), 10 East 14 Street, New York, N. Y. (defunct).

    F69 For you and me.
        Molineux, 1896 (Collection of part songs and choruses
        for male voices, no. 966).

Music Press, Inc.
    see: Presser.

New Music Editions.
    see: Associated Music Publishers.
       Presser.

New York Public Library, Lincoln Center, 111 Amsterdam Avenue,
New York, N. Y., 10023.

    C15 Calcium light night (1898–1907); arr., chamber orchestra.
       Photostatic reproduction of Henry Cowell's arrangement, 1936.
       Not available for sale or loan. Original manuscript
       held by the Library of Congress.

Peer International, 1619 Broadway, New York, N. Y., 10019.

    A44 All the way around and back.
       Peer (to be published).

    C38 The celestial country.
       Peer (to be published).

    C62 Circus band, chorus & orchestra.
       Peer (to be published).

    D28 December.
       Peer, 1963 (pl. nos. 580-12 [score], 580a-1 [parts], 812-2
       [choral parts]).

    F57 Flag song.
       Peer, 1968.

    F93 From the steeples.
       Peer, 1965 (pl. no. 980-8).

    G63 The gong on the hook and ladder.
       Peer, 1960.

    H75 Holidays.
       Decoration Day: Peer, 196?. Score to be published; parts on rent.
       Thanksgiving: Peer, 196?. Rental.

    I29 Ilmenau: Over all the treetops.
       Peer, 1952.

    I41 In re con moto et al.
       Peer, 1968.

    L31 Largo, piano, clarinet & violin.
       Southern Music Publishing Co., 1953.

L32 Largo, violin & piano.
　　Southern Music Publishing Co., 1967 (pl. no. 1064-6).
　　　Paul Zukofsky, ed. This movement is from the Pre-first
　　　violin sonata (S748).

L33 Largo risoluto, piano quintet, no. 1.
　　Peer, 1961 (pl. no. 583-4).

L34 Largo risoluto, piano quintet, no. 2.
　　Peer, 1961 (pl. no. 598-3).

L64 Let there be light.
　　Peer, 1967 (score pl. no. 592-2, parts pl. no. 592-1).

L65 Let there be light, men's voices & organ.
　　Peer, 1955 (pl. no. 311-2).

L66 Let there be light, mixed voices & organ.
　　Peer, 1955 (pl. no. 312-2).

L82 Lincoln, the great commoner, voice & piano.
　　Peer, 1952.

N53 The new river, mixed voices & chamber orchestra.
　　Peer (to be published). Henry Cowell, ed.

N54 The new river, voice & piano.
　　Peer (to be published).

N68 A night song.
　　Peer, 1952.

O65 Orchestral set, no. 2.
　　Peer, 196?. Rental.

O96 Over the pavements.
　　Peer, 1954.

Q11 Quartet, strings, no. 1.
　　Peer, 1963 (pl. no. 724-28).

Q2 Quartet, strings, no. 2.
　　Peer, 1954 (pl. no. 293-26).

R15 The rainbow.
　　Peer, 1959 (pl. no. 490-7).

R64 Robert Browning overture.
　　Peer, 1959 (pl. no. 351-87). Parts on rent. Lou Harrison &
　　　Henry Cowell, eds.

S12 Sacred songs.
　　Peer, 1961.

S54 Set, bass & piano quintet.
    Hymn: Peer, 1966 (pl. no. 1060-41).
    Scherzo: Peer, 1958.
    The innate: Peer, 1967 (pl. no. 1070-4).

S553 Set, orchestra, no. 3, 1C35.
    Adagio sostenuto: Peer (to be published).

S73 A son of a gambolier; arr., band.
    Peer, 1962 (pl. no. 727-16). Jonathan Elkus, arr.

S741 Sonata, piano, no. 1.
    Peer, 1954 (pl. no. 258-5).

S751 Sonata, violin & piano, no. 1.
    Peer, 1953 (pl. no. 125-35).

S788 Songs, 6AF (10 songs).
    Peer, 1953.

S79 Songs, 6AG (12 songs).
    Peer, 1954.

S791 Songs, 6AH (14 songs).
    Peer, 1955.

S793 Songs, 6AJ (9 songs).
    Peer, 1956.

S794 Songs, 6AK (13 songs).
    Peer, 1958.

S991 Symphony, no. 1, D minor.
    Peer (to be published). Parts on rent.

S992 Symphony, no. 2.
    Southern Music Publishing Co., 1951. Parts on rent.

T44 They are there!, unison chorus & orchestra.
    Peer, 1961 (pl. no. 625-17).

T45 They are there!, voice & piano.
    Peer, 1961 (pl. no. 607-6).

T67 Tone roads, no. 1.
    Peer, 1949 (pl. no. 18-7).

T69 Tone roads, no. 2.
    Peer, 1952.

T84 Trio, piano & strings.
    Peer, 1955 (pl. no. 303-27).

U54 The unanswered question.
Southern Music Publishing Co., 1953 (pl. no. 256-5).

V97 Vote for names, voice(s) & 3 pianos.
Peer, 1968 (pl. no. 2014-2). Version for voice & piano.
Peer, 1968 (pl. no. 2014-3). Version for voices & 3 pianos.

W58 When the moon is on the wave.
Peer, 1958.

Pepper (J. W.) & Son, Inc., 231 North 3d Street, Philadelphia, Pa., 19106.

I61 Intercollegiate march.
Pepper, 1896. Out of print.

Presser (Theodore) Co., Presser Place, Bryn Mawr, Pa., 19010.

A23 Adeste fideles in an organ prelude.
Music Press, 1949 (Music Press organ series MP-601).
Published with V31.

A63 The anti-abolitionist riots.
Mercury, 1949 (pl. no. 189).

C14 Calcium light night (1898-1907).
New Music, v.24 [i.e., v.26] no. 4, incorrectly issued under the
title The gong on the hook and ladder. Withdrawn.

C45 Chanson de Florian.
Mercury, 1950.

E39 An election.
Mercury, 1950.

G33 General William Booth's entrance into heaven, voice & piano.
New Music, v.9, no.1, 1935. Out of print.

G36 General William Booth's entrance into heaven;
arr., chamber orchestra.
Merion, 1963. Arranged by John J. Becker. Rental.

H33 Harvest home chorales.
Mercury, 1949 (pl. no. C5, C6, C7). Henry Cowell, ed. Out of print.
Mercury, 1963 (MC-446). Henry Cowell, ed.

L74 The light that is felt.
Mercury, 1950.

L81 Lincoln, the great commoner.
New Music Edition, 1932 (Orchestra series, no. 1).
Reprinted in New Music, v.26, no.2, January 1953.

P96 Protests.
New Music, v.21, no. 1, 1947. Out of print.

P97 Psalm 14.
Mercury, 195?.

P972 Psalm 24.
Mercury, 1955 (pl. no. MC155-8).

P973, P975, P977, P979: These Psalm settings, supposedly issued by
Mercury during the 1950's, are not available from Presser.
Further information has not been determined in correspondence
with the publishers.

P978 Psalm 100.
Mercury (?), 195–.
Presser (to be published).

P98 Psalm 150.
Mercury (?), 195–.
Presser (to be published).

S56 Set for theatre or chamber orchestra.
New Music Editions, 1932 (Orchestra series, no. 5). Score
reprinted by New Music Editions in 1948. Parts on rent.

S71 Some southpaw pitching.
Mercury, 1949 (pl. no. 190).

S753 Sonata, violin & piano, no. 3.
New Music Editions, 1951, v.34, no.2. To be reprinted.
Merion, 1967 (pl. no. 144-40019). Edited by Sol Babitz and
Ingolf Dahl.

S783 Songs, 6AC (34 songs).
New Music Editions, October 1933, v.7, no.1.
Merion, 1963 (pl. no. 441-41006). Order of songs changed.

S784 Songs, 6AD (18 songs; actually 19 songs).
New Music, October 1935, v.9, no.1.
Merion, 1964 (pl. no. 441-41007). Correction in title total
of songs made.

S786 Songs, 6AE (4 songs for low voice).
Mercury, 1950, 1933.

T53 Three-page sonata, piano.
Mercury, 1949 (pl. no. 191).

T54 Three places in New England.
Birchard, 1935; Mercury, 195?.
Merion, 1969.

T95 Turn ye, turn ye.
Mercury, 1955 (pl. no. MC-170).
Merion, 1969.

T96 Twenty-two.
New Music Editions, 1947. Out of print.

V31 Variations on America, organ.
Music Press, 1949 (Music Press organ series MP-601)
published with A23.

V32 Variations on America; arr., band.
Merion, 1968 (pl. no. 145-40006).

V33 Variations on America; arr., orchestra.
Merion, 1964 (pl. no. 446-41010). Parts on rent.

Schirmer (G.), 509 Fifth Avenue, New York, N. Y., 10017.

S752 Sonata, violin & piano, no. 2.
Schirmer, 1951 (pl. no. 42051).

S78 Songs, 6AA (114 songs).
Schirmer, 1921. Privately printed; permanently out of print.

Shepard (Th. G.), New Haven, Conn. (defunct).

B44 The bells of Yale.
Shepard, 1903 (Yale melodies, p.88–93).

Southern Music Publishing Co., 1619 Broadway, New York, N. Y., 10019.
see: Peer.

Summy-Birchard Publishing Co., 1834 Ridge Avenue, Evanston, Ill., 60204.
see: Presser.

Woodward (Willis) & Co., 842 Broadway, N. Y. (defunct).

W71 William Will.
Woodward, 1896.

Yale Courant.

S42 A Scotch lullaby.
1896, v.33, no.5, p.125–127.

S772 A song of Mory's.
    1897, v.33, no.9, p.280–281.

Lost, incomplete or unfinished:

A19, A27, A41, A49, A62, A93, A95, B36, B47, B82, B96, C48, C53, C55, C56, C57, C73, D17, D37, D38, D68, D75, F21, F97, F98, F99, G32, G56, G58, G79, H39, H47, H73, H74, H99, I16, I35, J65, J93, K99, L72, M321, M326, M334, M335, M34, M43, M52, M53, M66, M99, N69, O13, O62, O64, O66, O97, O98, P27, P35, P62, P63, P64, P66, P67, P68, P76, P86, P87, P88, P89, P91, P911, P912, P913, P914, P915, P917, P971, Q12, R14, R88, S37, S51, S58, S59, S591, S592, S66, S743, S746, S747, S755, S764, S766, S767, S92, S96, S98, T25, T43, T64, T68, T74, T83, U58, V57, V94, V95, V97, W31, Y16.

Unpublished (extant & complete?):

A42, A43, A45, B38, B46, C22, C24, C39, C46, C59, C63, C64, C66, C85, C86, C95, D36, D77, D79, D81, E38, E53, E56, E96, F23, F94, F95, F96, G34, G72, H34, H43, H53, H97, I11, I12, I13, I15, I18, I36, I39, I62, I63, J94, L35, L36, L53, L73, L75, L78, L86, L91, L92, M19, M23, M24, M31, M322, M323, M324, M325, M331, M332, M333, M337, M338, M339, M68, M96, N35, N55, O11, O12, O14, O47, O58, P28, P65 [recorded], P85, P916, P974, R75, R94, R95, S44, S45, S531, S541, S552, S553, S554, S556, S557, S57, S61, S63, S68, S732, S761, S748, S762, S763, S765, S773, S774, S85, S95, S9942, S9943, T13, T37, T55, T63, T77, V34, W23, W26, W56, W63, W64, W84, Y39, Y43.

Medium Index

Medium classifications below are designed to register the works of Ives as specifically as possible. Some variations from the subject headings of the Library of Congress thus become necessary in order to allow as much latitude in the classifications as Ives allowed in his music. Secular choruses do not include liturgical texts, and the expression of religious sentiments has not automatically qualified a work for a sacred category.

Band music:
   C59, C85, F21, H73, I61, M31, M34, O96, R94, S37, S66, S73, T74, V33.

Cantatas:
   C38.

Choruses, Sacred:
   B36, B46, B47, C57, E96, G56, I13, K99, L72, L86, M86, O13, P97, P971, P973, P974, P975, P978, P979, P98, S45, T25, V57.

Choruses, Sacred, with organ:
   E13, G58, L73.

Choruses, Sacred (Mixed voices, 4 pts.):
   C73, P972, P973, P974, P976.

Choruses, Sacred (Mixed voices, 4 pts.) with organ:
   P977.

Choruses, Secular:
   A62, B82, C46, C95, D36, H97, H99, P28, T43, W23.

Choruses, Secular, with band:
   G34.

Choruses, Secular, with orchestra:
   A41, E38, H43, J65, M24, S51, S531, S68.

Choruses, Secular, with 2 pianos:
O57.

Choruses, Secular (Men's voices, 4 pts.) unaccompanied:
A27, F69, I16, M99, N35, P27, S772.

Choruses, Secular (Men's voices, 4 pts.) with instr. ensemble:
L64.

Choruses, Secular (Men's voices, 4 pts.) with orchestra:
L81, S63.

Choruses, Secular (Men's voices, 4 pts.) with organ:
L64, S63.

Choruses, Secular (Men's voices, 4 pts.) with piano:
B44, L65, O14.

Choruses, Secular (Mixed voices, 4 pts.) unaccompanied:
S85, Y39.

Choruses, Secular (Mixed voices, 4 pts.) with chamber orchestra:
N53.

Choruses, Secular (Mixed voices, 4 pts.) with instr. ensemble:
H33, L64.

Choruses, Secular (Mixed voices, 4 pts.) with orchestra:
L81.

Choruses, Secular (Mixed voices, 4 pts.) with organ:
L66, T95.

Choruses, Secular (Mixed voices, 4 pts.) with piano:
L66, T95.

Choruses, Secular (Mixed voices, 7 pts.) with instr. ensemble:
C62.

Choruses, Secular (Unison voices) with instr. ensemble:
D28, L76.

Choruses, Secular (Unison voices) with orchestra:
T44.

Choruses, Secular (Unison voices) with piano:
S52, T45.

Choruses, Secular (Women's voices, 4 pts.) with orchestra:
L81.

Cornet music (2 cornets) with piano:
P76.

Instrumental ensembles:
A44, C14, C61, O47.

Operas:
J93.

Orchestral music:
A47, A49, A95, C14, C15, C41, C48, C61, C63, C632, C67, D17, D75, E53,
F93, G32, G36, G63, H39, H74, H75, I612, L47, L76, M23, M321, M322,
M323, M324, M325, M326, M43, N69, O64, O65, O66, O97, 098, P67,
P68, P79, P85, R14, R64, R93, S552, S556, S557, S56, S57, S58, S59, S591,
S592, S98, S991, S992, S993, S994, S9942, T54, T67, T68, T69, U54, U58,
V32, V34, W58, Y16, Y17.

Organ music:
A19, A23, C24, C53, F95, F96, I62, M52, M53, P66, P86, P87, P88, P89,
P91, P9111, P912, P913, P914, P915, P917, S732, T64, V31, V94, V95.

Organ with chamber orchestra:
P62.

Piano music:
A63, C395, C59, C64, I63, M331, M332, M333, M334, M335, M336,
M337, M338, M339, M66, N55, P63, P96, Q1, S71, S741, S742, S743,
S92, S9943, T13, T53, T77, T96, W26.

Piano music (4 hands):
D79.

Piano music (2 pianos):
B96, C56, Q1.

Piano quintets:
H19, I41, L33, L34, S54.

Piano trios:
T84.

Piano with orchestra:
S56.

Quartets (organ, trombone, 2 violins):
P916.

Songs with band:
G34.

Songs with instr. ensemble:
S769.

Songs with chamber orchestra:
L36.

Songs with orchestra:
C66, R15.

Songs with organ:
S769, W31.

Songs with piano:
A14, A25, A26, A41b, A43, A46, A48, A52, A61, A86, A87, A88, A92,
A93, A94, B38, B48, C13, C18, C22, C23, C39, C45, C47, C54, C57, C65,
C69, C86, C88, D29, D61, D68, D74, D77, D78, D81, E23, E39, E41, E56,
E93, E94, F22, F23, F24, F29, F57, F74, F94, G33, G57, G72, G76, G78,
H29, H34, H44, H45, H53, H67, H72, H82, H98, I11, I12, I14, I15, I17,
I18, I29, I33, I35, I37, I38, I39, I42, I43, I44, I45, I46, I58, J94, K11,
L35, L37, L53, L74, L75, L77, L78, L82, L88, L91, L92, L94, M19, M25,
M29, M35, M54, M67, M68, M69, M96, M97, M98, N31, N54, M67, N68,
N71, N73, O11, O12, O43, O44, O45, O55, O59, O61, O62, P22, P35, P43,
P61, P74, P918, Q6, R16, R38, R39, R42, R43, R68, R75, R78, R85, R95,
S12, S42, S43, S44, S47, S48, S52, S61, S62, S64, S65, S67, S69, S72,
S761, S762, S763, S764, S765, S766, S767, S768, S771, S773, S774, S78,
S781, S782, S783, S784, S785, S786, S787, S788, S79, S791, S792, S793,
S794, S795, S81, S82, S83, S84, S95, S96, S97, T19, T37, T41, T42, T45,
T46, T48, T52, T55, T62, T63, T65, T66, T97, V97, W14, W17, W24,
W25, W32, W42, W52, W56, W57, W59, W61, W62, W63, W64, W65,
W71, W84, W92, W93, Y43.

Songs with piano (2 pianos):
O57.

Songs with piano (3 pianos):
V97.

String quartets:
F97, F98, F99, G79, P64, Q11, Q12, Q2.

String-orchestra music:
C55, S541.

Trios (piano, clarinet, violin):
L31, T83.

Trios (piano, saxophone, trumpet):
S554.

Trumpet with organ:
S746.

Unknown or unspecified instrumentation:
    D37, D38, H47, R88.

Violin and piano music:
    A45, L32, P914, S747, S748, S751, S752, S753, S754, S755.

Vocal quartets:
    A42, E12.

Vocal quartets with organ:
    L73.

Chronological Index

The following list registers works by Ives under the year of completion. Compositions whose chronology is not firmly established are placed under the latest probable date. Arrangements made which were not requested or supervised by the composer appear at the conclusion of this index, along with works for which no date can reasonably be established.

1886

M66	Minuet, piano, op. 4
S37	Schoolboy march, band, op. 1

1887

C46	Chant, op. 2, no. 2
H74	Holiday quickstep, orchestra
H97	Hymn, 5C1
N55	New year's dance, piano
P76	Polonaise, 2 cornets & piano
P974	Psalm 42
S66	Slow march on Adeste fideles, band
V94	Voluntary, organ, 3D1, C minor
V95	Voluntary, organ, 3D2, F major

1888

H45	Hear my prayer, O Lord
H73	Holiday quickstep, band
S65	Slow march, voice & piano
S761	Song, 6B10b

1889

A49	The American woods overture
A86	At parting
P63	Piece, piano, 3B3, G minor
V34	Variations on Jerusalem the golden, organ
Y39	The year's at spring

1890

A14	Abide with me
B46	Benedictus, 5C9, E major
F22	Far from my heav'nly home
I13	I think of thee, my God
M321	March, orchestra, 1C3, no. 1
M331	March, piano, 3B4, no. 1, B flat & F
T95	Turn ye, turn ye

1891

B47	Benedictus, 5C13, G major
C57	Christ, our passover . . .
C73	Communion service
C86	Country celestial
C95	Crossing the bar
F21	Fantasia on Jerusalem the golden, band
G56	Gloria in excelsis
I35	In a mountain spring
P64	Piece, string quartet, 2B1a
S762	Song, 6B13a, G major
S85	Stars of the summer night

1892

A19	Adagio, organ, 3D7, F major
A43	All love that has not friendship . . .
B36	Be thou, O God, exalted high . . .
B82	Bread of the world
E13	Easter carol
E96	Experimental canticle phrases
G58	God of my life
H72	Holder klingt der Vogelsang . . .
I61	Intercollegiate march, band
I62	Interludes for hymns, organ
L78	Like unfathomable lakes
M19	Magnificat
M332	March, piano, 3B5, no. 2, C & F
M333	March, piano, 3B6, no. 3, C & F

M337	March, piano, 3B10, no. 5, B flat & D
O13	O God, my heart is fixed
P86	Postlude, organ, 3D4, F major
R68	Rock of ages
S45	Search me, O Lord
S763	Song, 6B14b
V31	Variations on America, organ
W57	When stars are in the quiet skies
W59	When the waves softly sigh . . .

1893

C22	Canon: Not only in my lady's eyes
C24	Canzonetta, organ, 3D8, F major
H34	Has she need of monarch's swaying wand . . .
I37	In autumn
L72	Life of the world
M323	March, orchestral, 1C5, no. 3, C & F
M334	March, piano, 3B7, no. 3a
M338	March, piano, 3B11, no. 5a, C & G
M52	Melody, organ, 3D9, E flat
S769	Song for a harvest season
T41	There is a certain garden . . .

1894

C23	Canon: Oh, the days are gone
C62	Circus band, chorus & orchestra
C63	Circus band, orchestra
C64	Circus band, piano
C65	Circus band, voice & piano
C66	Circus band, voice & piano; voice & orchestra
F23	Far in the wood
K11	Kären
L86	Lord God, thy sea is mighty . . .
M324	March, orchestra, 1C6, no. 3
M325	March, orchestra, 1C7, no. 4, C & F
M335	March, piano, 3B8, no. 3b
M336	March, piano, 3B9, no. 4
M86	Morning service
O45	The old mother, 6B20a
P43	A perfect day
R88	Royal rivals
S61	She is not fair to outward view . . .
V57	Vesper service

1895

F97	Fugue, string quartet, 2B2, B flat major
F98	Fugue, string quartet, 2B3, D major
F99	Fugue, string quartet, 2B4
I11	I hear a tone so wondrous rare . . .
I16	I wrote a rhyme . . .
I36	In April tide
I39	In my beloved's eyes
L53	Leise zieht durch mein Gemüth
L92	Love does not die
M322	March, orchestra, 1C4, no. 2, B flat & F
M97	My native land
N35	'Neath the elm trees . . .
N68	A night song
N71	A night thought
P85	Postlude, orchestra, 1B1, F major
S72	A son of a gambolier
S747	Sonata, violin & piano, pre-pre-no. 1
S82	Songs my mother taught me
T63	To love someone more dearly . . .
W25	Waltz, voice & piano
W93	The world's wanderers

1896

A27	Age of gold
A41	The all-enduring, chorus & orchestra
A41b	The all-enduring, voice & piano
A52	Amphion
B96	Burlesque storm
D37	Delta Kappa Epsilon sketch, 4A3
D38	Delta Kappa Epsilon spring show
F69	For you and me
F94	Frühlingslied
H47	Hell's bells
I43	In the alley
I63	Invention, piano, 3B14, D major
M31	March, band, 1D6, C & F
M339	March, piano, 3B13, no. 6, D & G
M35	Marie
O43	An old flame
O97	Overture, orchestra, 1B2, G minor
P27	Partsong, 5D9, B flat & D
P87	Postlude, organ, 3D12

P91	Prelude, organ, 3D10
P911	Prelude, organ, 3D11
P975	Psalm 54
Q11	Quartet, strings, no. 1
S42	A Scotch lullaby
S764	Song, 6B23a
T55	Through night and day
T74	Town, gown and state overture
W71	William Will

1897

A23	Adeste fideles in an organ prelude
B44	The bells of Yale
D36	Delta Kappa Epsilon
D77	Dream sweetly
D78	Dreams
D81	Du bist wie eine Blume
F95	Fugue, organ, 3D14, C minor
F96	Fugue, organ, 3D15, E flat major
G57	God bless and keep them
G79	Greek fugue in four keys, string quartet
H53	Her gown was of vermilion silk
I42	In summer fields
K99	Kyrie eleison
M326	March, orchestra, 1C9, no. 6
M54	Memories
N73	No more
O12	O danke nicht für diese Lieder . . .
P28	Pass the can along
P88	Postlude, organ, 3D12
P89	Postlude for Thanksgiving service, organ
P915	Prelude for Thanksgiving service, organ
P972	Psalm 24
P973	Psalm 25
P976	Psalm 67
S732	Sonata, organ, 3D16
S772	A song of Mory's
S95	The sun shines hot on quarry walls . . .
W92	The world's highway

1898

A42	All-forgiving
A48	Alone upon the housetops

A62	Anthem, chorus, 5C32
B38	Because of you
C58	A Christmas carol
D75	Down east overture
F57	Flag song
I17	Ich grolle nicht
J94	Judges' walk
L35	The lark will make her hymn . . .
L91	Love divine
M99	My sweet Jeannette
O11	O breath of early morning . . .
O14	O maiden fair
P98	Psalm 150
R78	Rosamunde
S58	Set of overtures
S771	A song—for anything
S991	Symphony, no. 1, D minor
T37	Thee I love
W64	Wie Melodien zieht es mir

1899

C38	The celestial country. English
F47	Forward into light
G72	Grace
I12	I knew and loved a maid . . .
I15	I went along the road
L88	Die Lotosblume
M34	March for Dewey Day, band
M96	My life has grown so dear to me . . .
N67	Night of frost in May
P916	Prelude on Abide with me, organ
P971	Psalm 23
P978	Psalm 100
S766	Song, 6B34c
W56	When the spring grows old . . .
Y16	Yale-Princeton football game

1900

A46	Allegro, voice & piano
B48	Berceuse
I18	Ich konnte heute nicht schlafen
O46	The old mother, 6B36b
O55	Omens and oracles
P914	Prelude, violin & piano

P979	Psalm 135
R75	Romanzo di Central Park
S746	Sonata, trumpet & organ
T25	Te Deum
W61	Where the eagle
W63	Who knows the light . . .
W65	Wiegenlied
W84	Wohl wanchen Rosenzweig

1901

C45	Chanson de Florian
C53	Children's day parade
C54	The children's hour
E41	Elégie
F93	From the steeples
I14	I travelled among unknown men
L64	Let there be light
L65	Let there be light. Piano-vocal score.
M53	Memorial slow march, organ
M98	My native land, 6B38c
P66	Piece for communion service, organ
P912	Prelude, organ, 3D23
P913	Prelude, organ, 3D24
P917	Preludes, organ, 3D25
P977	Psalm 90
Q6	Qu'il m'irait bien
S765	Song, 6B38a, E flat major
T64	Toccata, organ, 3D21
W31	Watchman

1902

A93	Autumn, 6B40e
C85	Country band march
D17	Danbury Fair skit
D79	Drum corps or scuffle
E56	The ending year
H29	Harpalus
H99	Hymn anthem on Abide with me
I29	Ilmenau: Over all the treetops
L31	Largo, piano, clarinet & violin
M67	Mirage
R85	Rough wind
S59	Set of ragtime pieces, orchestra, 1C16
S67	Slugging a vampire

T19	Tarrant moss
T42	There is a lane
T43	There is no unbelief
W17	Walking
W42	Weil' auf mir

1903

O47	An old song deranged
R14	Ragtime dance, orchestra
S44	The sea of sleep
S748	Sonata, violin & piano, pre-no. 1
S767	Song, 6B41b
S774	Songbook C
T83	Trio, piano, clarinet & violin

1904

A95	Autumn landscape from Pine Mountain
G32	The General Slocum, July 1904
L74	The light that is felt, medium voice & piano
M23	Major Andre overture
O64	Orchard House overture
O98	Overture and march "1776," orchestra
S591	Set of ragtime pieces, orchestra, 1C16

1905

P62	Piece, organ & chamber orchestra, 1C23
P67	Piece on Beautiful river, orchestra
P68	Piece on Watchman, orchestra
Q12	Quartet, strings, pre-no. 2
R94	Runaway horse on Main Street
T53	Three-page sonata, piano

1906

A44	All the way around and back
C13	The cage
C41	Central Park in the dark
L33	Largo risoluto, piano quintet, no. 1
P79	The pond
S754	Sonata, violin & piano, no. 4
U54	The unanswered question

1907

A45	Allegro, violin & piano
C14	Calcium light night (1898–1907)
E53	Emerson overture

H19	Hallowe'en
J93	The judgement hall
L47	A lecture
N53	The new river
P61	Pictures
R93	The ruined river
S46	The see'r
S57	Set of cartoons or take-offs
S69	Soliloquy
S83	The south wind
S84	Spring song
T13	Take-offs
T52	Those evening bells

1908

A63	The anti-abolitionist riots
A94	Autumn, 6B45
L34	Largo risoluto, piano quintet, no. 2
L76	Like a sick eagle
N31	Nature's way
S54	Set, bass & piano quintet
S71	Some southpaw pitching
S768	Song—a poem of Kipling?
W14	The waiting soul
W58	When the moon is on the wave
Y17	Yale-Princeton game, August 1907

1909

D68	Don't you see . . .
F24	A farewell to land
R95	Runaway horse on Main Street, voice & piano
S51	Serenity
S751	Sonata, violin & piano, no. 1
S992	Symphony, no. 2
T65	Tolerance

1910

E94	Evidence
H39	Hawthorne overture
M68	Mists, 6B47
M69	Mists, 6B47a
P96	Protests
S741	Sonata, piano, no. 1

S752   Sonata, violin & piano, no. 2
S773   Songbook B

1911

G63   The gong on the hook and ladder
L36   The last reader
R42   Requiem
S56   Set for theatre or chamber orchestra
S993   Symphony, no. 3
T67   Tone roads, no. 1
T84   Trio, piano & strings
W26   Waltz-rondo, piano

1912

C18   The camp meeting
H33   Harvest home chorales
L81   Lincoln, the great commoner
M43   Matthew Arnold overture
R64   Robert Browning overture
S552   Set, orchestra, no. 2, 1C32
S92   Studies, piano
T96   Twenty-two
V97   Vote for names

1913

D28   December
H67   His exaltation
H75   Holidays
T41   In re con moto et al
O96   Over the pavements
S63   Slants, or Christian and pagan
W23   Walt Whitman
W32   Watchman, voice & piano

1914

C55   Chorale for strings in quarter-tones
C56   Chorale for strings in quarter-tones, 2 pianos
G33   General William Booth's entrance into heaven
G34   General William Booth's entrance into heaven, mixed voices
        & band
M24   The majority
R15   The rainbow
S68   Sneak thief
S753   Sonata, violin & piano, no. 3
T54   Three places in New England

1915

C47	Charlie Rutlage
L75	Light-winged smoke
O65	Orchestral set, no. 2
S592	1776
S742	Sonata, piano, no. 2
S755	Sonata, violin & piano, no. 5
T48	Thoreau
T69	Tone roads, no. 3

1916

A88	At parting
C395	The celestial railroad
I58	The innate
S994	Symphony, no. 4

1917

H43	He is there! May 30, 1917, chorus & orchestra
H44	He is there! May 30, 1917, voice & piano
I38	In Flanders field
T46	The things our father loved
T66	Tom sails away

1918

S553	Set, orchestra, no. 3, 1C35

1919

A26	Afterglow
C59	Chromâtimelôdtune
C88	Cradle song
D74	Down east
S52	Serenity, unison voices & piano
T62	To Edith
T68	Tone roads, no. 2

1920

A92	August
C69	The collection
D29	December, voice & piano
E38	An election
F29	La fède
G76	Grantchester
L77	Like a sick eagle, voice & piano
L94	Luck and work
M29	Maple leaves

O44	Old home day
O59	On the counter
R38	Religion
S47	The see'r, voice & piano
S48	September
S554	Set, orchestra, no. 6, 1C38

1921

A61	Ann Street
A87	At sea
D61	Disclosure
E39	An election, voice & piano
G78	The greatest man
H82	The Housatonic at Stockbridge
H98	Hymn, 6B62
I33	Immortality
I45	Incantation
I46	The Indians
L37	The last reader
L82	Lincoln, the great commoner, voice & piano
M25	The majority, voice & piano
N54	The new river, voice & piano
O61	One, two, three
P22	Paracelsus
P918	Premonitions
R16	The rainbow, voice & piano
R39	Remembrance
R43	Resolution
S62	The side show
S64	Slants, or Christian and pagan, voice & piano
S97	The swimmers
T77	Transcriptions from Emerson
T97	Two little flowers
W24	Walt Whitman, voice & piano
W52	West London
W62	The white gulls

1922

A25	Aeschylus and Sophocles
C48	Charlie Rutlage, orchestra
S556	Set, orchestra, no. 5, 1C37
S557	Set, orchestra, no. 6, 1C38
S98	The swimmers, orchestra

1923

O57	On the antipodes
O62	The one way
P35	Peaks
Y43	Yellow leaves

1924

| Q1 | Pieces, piano (quarter-tone) |

1925

E23	Edie's carol
J65	Johnny Poe
S43	A sea dirge

1926

| O66 | Orchestral set, no. 3 |
| S96 | Sunrise |

1927

| S743 | Sonata, piano, no. 3 |

1928

| U58 | Universe symphony |

1929

| I44 | In the mornin' |

1936

| C15 | Calcium light night (1898–1907); arr., chamber orchestra |

1942

| T44 | They are there!, chorus & orchestra |
| T45 | They are there!, voice & piano |

Undated work

| L32 | Largo, violin & piano |

Arrangements

C61	Chromâtimelôdtune; arr., chamber orchestra
C67	Circus band, voice & piano; arr., orchestra
G36	General William Booth's entrance into heaven; arr., chamber orchestra
I612	Intercollegiate march, band; arr., orchestra
N69	A night song; arr., orchestra
S541	Set, bass & piano quintet. Hymn; arr., string orchestra
S73	A son of a gambolier; arr., band

S9942   Symphony, no. 4. Fugue; arr., orchestra
S9943   Symphony, no. 4. Fugue; arr., piano
V32   Variations on America, organ; arr., band
V33   Variations on America, organ; arr., orchestra

Index of Arrangers, Poets and Librettists

The following index includes the names of poets whose texts Ives has set, as well as editors and arrangers of those works which are included in the bibliography.

Aldrich, Thomas Bailey, 1836–1907:
M29.
Alford, Henry, 1810–1871:
C38, F74, H33.
Allmers, Hermann, 1821–1902:
I42.
Ariosto, Ludovico, 1474–1533:
F29.
Arnold, Matthew, 1822–1888:
W52.
Becker, John J.:
G36.
Bélanger:
R78.
Bellamann, Henry, 1882– :
P35, Y43.
Bernard of Cluny, Saint, 12th century:
C38.
Bernhoff, John:
I15.

Bible:
B36, B46, C57, M19, O13, P97,
P971, P972, P973, P974, P975,
P976, P977, P978, P979, P98,
S45.
Bixby, Dr. James T., 1943–1921:
R38, T43.
Bowring, John, 1792–1872:
W31, W32.
Brady, Nicholas, 1659–1726:
H45, O13.
Brewster, Judge Lyman D.:
A41, A41b, M23.
Brooke, Rupert, 1887–1915:
G76.
Browning, Robert, 1812–1889:
P22, Y39.
Bulwer-Lytton, 1803–1873:
W57.
Burgess, George, 1809-1866:
H33.

Phonorecord Index

Alco 101/2.   4s.   12in.   78rpm.
   S752   In the barn.
   S752   The revival.
   Performers: Sol Babitz, violin; Ingolf Dahl, piano.
American Recording Society ARS-27.   2s.   10in.   33rpm.   R53-821.
   T54   Three places in New England.
   Performers: American Recording Society Orchestra; Walter Hendl,
      conductor.
   With: Concerto for violin, by R. McBride.
American Recording Society ARS-116.   2s.   12in.   33rpm.
   T54   Three places in New England.
   Performers: American Recording Society Orchestra; Walter Hendl,
      conductor.
   With: Concerto for violin, by R. McBride.—Rounds, by D. Diamond.—
      Short symphony, by H. Swanson.
Artist 1404.
   see: Artist LP-100.
Artist JS-13.   8s.   12in.   78rpm.
   see: Artist LP-100.

Artist LP-100. 2s. 12in. 33rpm.

>Four American landscapes.
>
>T54   The Housatonic at Stockbridge.
>
>Performers: Janssen Symphony Orchestra; Werner Janssen, conductor.
>
>With: Quiet city, by A. Copland.—Ancient desert drone, by
>   H. Cowell.—Dance in the place Congro, by H. Gilbert.
>
>x: Artist 1404. x: Artist JS-13.

CBS 72630.

>Q11   Quartet no. 1.
>
>Q2   Quartet no. 2.
>
>Performers: Juilliard String Quartet.

Cambridge 804. 2s. 12in. 33rpm. R63-1366.

>A61   Ann Street.
>
>C13   The cage.
>
>E39   An election.
>
>F24   A farewell to land.
>
>G33   General William Booth's entrance into heaven.
>
>H19   Hallowe'en.
>
>I17   Ich grolle nicht.
>
>I46   The Indians.
>
>O61   One, two, three.
>
>O96   Over the pavements.
>
>P79   The pond.
>
>R15   The rainbow.
>
>R38   Religion.
>
>S54   Hymn; largo cantabile.
>
>T53   Three-page sonata.
>
>T67   Tone roads, no. 1.
>
>T69   Tone roads, no. 3.
>
>Performers: Boston Chamber Ensemble; Luise Vosgerchian, piano;
>   Corrine Curry, mezzo-soprano; Harold Farberman, conductor.
>
>x: Cambridge CRS-1804st.

Cambridge CRS-1804st. 2s. 12in. 33rpm. A63-1367.

>see: Cambridge 804.

Columbia 17139D. 2s. 10in. 78rpm.

>P976   Psalm 67.
>
>Performers: Madrigal Singers; Lehmann Engel, conductor.
>
>With: Choral etude, by W. Schuman.

Columbia 72535/9D. 10s. 12in. 78rpm.

>S741   Piano sonata no. 1.
>
>S742   Piano sonata no. 2.
>
>Performer: John Kirkpatrick.

Columbia CLPS-1008. 2[?]s. 12[?]in. 33rpm.

C47   Charlie Rutlage.

Performer: Randolph Symonette, bass.

Other contents not determined.

Columbia D3S-783. 6s. 12in. 33rpm. R68-2980.

The four symphonies of Charles Ives.

S991   Symphony no. 1.

S992   Symphony no. 2.

S993   Symphony no. 3.

S994   Symphony no. 4.

Performers: Philadelphia Orchestra; Eugene Ormandy, conductor (S991); New York Philharmonic; Leonard Bernstein, conductor (S992, S993); American Symphony Orchestra; Schola Cantorum of New York; Leopold Stokowski, conductor (S994).

Columbia KL-5489. 2s. 12in. 33rpm. R60-1175.

S992   Symphony no. 2.

Performers: New York Philharmonic; Leonard Bernstein, conductor.

x: Columbia KS-6155st.

Columbia KS-6155st. 2s. 12in. 33rpm. R60-1176.

see: Columbia KL-5489.

Columbia ML-2169. 2s. 10in. 33rpm.

S752   Violin sonata no. 2.

Performers: Patricia Travers, violin; Otto Herz, piano.

With: Duo for violin & piano, by S. Sessions.

Columbia ML-4250. 2s. 12in. 33rpm.

S742   Piano sonata no. 2.

Performer: John Kirkpatrick.

Columbia ML-4490. 2s. 12in. 33rpm. R53-26.

S741   Piano sonata no. 1.

Performer: William Masselos.

Columbia ML-5496. 2s. 12in. 33rpm.

The organ in America.

V31   Variations on America.

Performer: E. Power Biggs.

With works by D. Michael, W. Brown, B. Yarnold, O. Shaw, P. Philie, W. Billings, W. Selby, J. Moller and J. Hewitt.

x: Columbia MS-6161st.

Columbia ML-6084. 2s. 12in. 33rpm. R64-1595.

T54   Three places in New England.

Performers: Philadelphia Orchestra; Eugene Ormandy, conductor.

With: Fanfare for the common man, by A. Copland.—A Lincoln portrait, by A. Copland.

x: Columbia MS-6684st.

Columbia ML-6175. 2s. 12in. 33rpm. R65-2594.

    S994   Symphony no. 4.

    Performers: American Symphony Orchestra; Schola Cantorum of New York; David Katz, José Serebrier, Hugh Ross, Leopold Stokowski, conductors.

    x: Columbia MS-6775st.

Columbia ML-6243. 2s. 12in. 33rpm. R66-2538.

    Bernstein conducts Charles Ives.

    C41   Central Park in the dark.

    H75   Decoration day.

    S993   Symphony no. 3.

    U54   The unanswered question.

    Performers: New York Philharmonic; Maurice Peress, piano; Leonard Bernstein, conductor.

    x: Columbia MS-6843st.

Columbia ML-6289. 2s. 12in. 33rpm. R66-2701.

    H75   The Fourth of July.

    S992   Symphony no. 2.

    Performers: New York Philharmonic; Seymour Lipkin and Leonard Bernstein, conductors.

    x: Columbia MS-6889st.

Columbia ML-6321. 2s. 12in. 33rpm. R66-3014.

    C62   Circus band.

    D28   December.

    G36   General William Booth enters into heaven.

    H33   Harvest home chorales.

    N53   The new river.

    P972   Psalm 24.

    S52   Serenity.

    Performers: Gregg Smith Singers; Ithaca College Choir; Texas Boys' Choir; Columbia Chamber Orchestra.

    x: Columbia MS-6921st.

Columbia ML-6415. 2s. 12in. 33rpm.

    The world of Charles Ives.

    H75   Washington's birthday.

    R64   Browning overture.

    T54   Three places in New England.

    Performers: Philadelphia Orchestra; Eugene Ormandy, conductor (T54); American Symphony Orchestra; Leopold Stokowski, conductor (R64); New York Philharmonic; Leonard Bernstein, conductor (H75).

    x: Columbia MS-7015st.

Columbia ML-6427. 2s. 12in. 33rpm. R67-3370.
Q11 Quartet no. 1.
Q2 Quartet no. 2.
Performers: Juilliard String Quartet.
x: Columbia MS-7027st.
Columbia MM-749. 10s. 12in. 78rpm.
S741 In the inn.
S742 Piano sonata no. 2.
Performer: John Kirkpatrick.
Columbia MM-987. [?]s. [?]in. 78rpm.
S752 Violin sonata no. 2.
Performers: Patricia Travers, violin; Otto Herz, piano.
With: Duo for violin & piano, by R. Sessions.
Columbia MS-6161st. 2s. 12in. 33rpm.
see: Columbia ML-5496.
Columbia MS-6684st. 2s. 12in. 33rpm. R64-1597.
see: Columbia ML-6084.
Columbia MS-6775st. 2s. 12in. 33rpm. R65-2595.
see: Columbia ML-6175.
Columbia MS-6843st. 2s. 12in. 33rpm. R66-2539.
see: Columbia ML-6243.
Columbia MS-6889st. 2s. 12in. 33rpm. R66-2702.
see: Columbia ML-6289.
Columbia MS-6921st. 2s. 12in. 33rpm. R66-3015.
see: Columbia ML-6321.
Columbia MS-7015st. 2s. 12in. 33rpm.
see: Columbia ML-6415.
Columbia MS-7027st. 2s. 12in. 33rpm. R67-3371.
see: Columbia ML-6427.
Columbia MS-7111st. 2s. 12in. 33rpm. R68-2555.
S991 Symphony no. 1.
T54 Three places in New England.
Performers: Philadelphia Orchestra; Eugene Ormandy, conductor.
Columbia MS-7147st. 2s 12in. 33rpm. R68-2983.
H75 Holidays.
Performers: New York Philharmonic; Leonard Bernstein, conductor.
Columbia MS-7192st. 2s. 12in. 33rpm.
S742 Piano sonata no. 2.
Performer: John Kirkpatrick.
Composers Recordings, Inc. CRI-150. 2s. 12in. 33rpm. R62-170.
S742 Piano sonata no. 2.
Performers: George Papa-stavrou, piano; Bonnie Lichter, flute.

Composers Recordings, Inc. CRI-163. 2s. 12in. 33rpm. R63-1244.
    C41   Central Park in the dark.
    H19   Hallowe'en.
    H75   Washington's birthday.
    P79   The pond.
    Performers: Imperial Philharmonic of Tokyo (H75); Oslo Philharmonic
    (C41, H19, P79); William Strickland, conductor.
    With: The lady of tearful regret, by W. Flanagan.
Composers Recordings, Inc. CRI-177. 2s. 12in. 33rpm. R64-250.
    H75   Thanksgiving.
    Performers: Iceland Symphony Orchestra; Iceland State Radio Chorus;
    William Strickland, conductor.
    With: Canon and fugue, by W. Riegger.—Concerto arabesque,
    by J. Becker.
Composers Recordings, Inc. CRI-180. 2s. 12in. 33rpm. R64-247.
    H75   The Fourth of July.
    Performers: Göteborg Symphony Orchestra; William Strickland,
    conductor.
    With: Concertino, by W. Piston.—Concertino, by J. Carpenter.
Composers Recordings, Inc. CRI-190SDst. 2s. 12in. 33rpm. R64-2405.
    H75   Washington's birthday.
    H75   Decoration day.
    H75   The Fourth of July.
    H75   Thanksgiving.
    Performers: Tokyo Imperial Orchestra (Washington's birthday);
    Finnish National Radio Symphony Orchestra (Decoration day);
    Göteborg Symphony Orchestra (The Fourth of July); Iceland
    Symphony Orchestra and State Radio Chorus (Thanksgiving);
    William Strickland, conductor.
    Note: Monaural version (withdrawn) issued as CRI-190.
Composers Recordings, Inc. CRI-196SDst. 2s. 12in. 33rpm. R66-50.
    R64   Robert Browning overture.
    Performers: Polish National Radio Orchestra; William Strickland,
    conductor.
    With: Symphony no. 1, by J. Beeson.
    Note: Monaural version (withdrawn) issued as CRI-196 (R66-52).
Concert Hall CHC-7. 6s. 12in. 78rpm.
    A88   At the river.
    C13   The cage.
    C54   The children's hour.
    C65   Circus band.
    C88   Cradle song.
    H29   Harpalus.

M67   Mirage.
M69   Mists.
N67   Night of frost in May.
N68   A night song.
O61   One, two, three.
R85   Rough wind.
S64   Vita.
T48   Thoreau.
T97   Two little flowers.
Performers: Ernest McChesney, tenor; Otto Herz, piano.
Decca DG-710.126st. 2s. 12in. 33rpm. R65-2983.
    see: Decca DL-10126.
Decca DL-10126. 2s. 12in. 33rpm. R65-2980.
T84   Trio, piano & strings.
Performers: Nieuw Amsterdam Trio.
With: Vitebsk, by A. Copland.—Nocturnes, by E. Bloch.
x: Decca DG-710.126st.
Desto 403. 2s. 12in. 33rpm.
T54   Three places in New England.
Performers: Vienna Symphony; Walter Hendl, conductor.
With: Appalachian spring, by A. Copland.
x: Desto DST-6403st.
Desto 6458/61st. 8s. 12in. 33rpm.
S741   Piano sonata no. 1.
S742   Piano sonata no. 2.
S92   Studies [selections].
T13   Take-offs.
T53   Three-page sonata.
Performer: Alan Mandel.
Desto D-411/2.
G33   General William Booth's entrance into heaven.
Performers: Donald Gramm, singer; pianist not verified.
Other contents not verified.
Desto DST-6403st. 2s. 12in. 33rpm. R65-1403.
    see: Desto 403.
Disc 775. [?]s. [?]in. 78rpm.
Q2   String quartet no. 2.
Performers: Walden String Quartet.
Duke. 4s. 12in. 33rpm.
Art song in America.
C23   Canon: Oh, the days are gone.
C47   Charlie Rutlage.
P22   Paracelsus.

Performers: John Kennedy Hanks, tenor; Ruth Friedberg, piano.
With works by E. Bacon, A. Copland, R. Harris, C. Daugherty,
  P. Bowles, R. L. Finney, S. Barber, P. Nordoff, Klenz, N. Dello Joio,
  E. MacDowell, G. W. Chadwick, C. M. Loeffler, R. Hageman,
  J. A. Carpenter, C. T. Griffes, W. Josten, V. Duke.
Educo 4006. 2s. 12in. 33rpm.
  Album of American songs.
  C47   Charlie Rutlage.
  W17   Walking.
  Performers: Donald Stenberg, baritone; Joann Crossman, piano.
  With works by J. A. Carpenter, C. T. Griffes, S. Barber, F. Hopkinson,
    B. Carr, S. Foster, A. Foote, G. W. Chadwick, S. Homer, A. Beach.
Everest 3118st. 2s. 12in. 33rpm.
  see: Everest 6118.
Everest 6118. 2s. 12in. 33rpm.
  Four American landscapes.
  T54   The Housatonic at Stockbridge.
  Performers: Los Angeles Orchestra; Werner Janssen, conductor.
  With: Quiet city, by A. Copland.—Ancient desert drone, by
    H. Cowell.—Dance in the place Congo, by H. Belknap.
  x: Everest 3118st.
Folkways FM-3344/5. 4s. 12in. 33rpm. R65-3027.
  A26   Afterglow
  A61   Ann Street
  C13   The cage.
  C23   Canon: Oh, the days are gone.
  C47   Charlie Rutlage.
  C54   The children's hour.
  C58   A Christmas carol.
  E39   An election.
  E93   Evening.
  F24   A farewell to land.
  G33   General William Booth enters into heaven.
  G76   Grantchester.
  I33   Immortality.
  I46   The Indians.
  L77   Like a sick eagle.
  L82   Lincoln, the great commoner.
  M25   The majority.
  M29   Maple leaves.
  M69   Mists.
  O57   On the antipodes.
  P22   Paracelsus.

R42   Requiem.
S48   September.
S52   Serenity.
S62   The side show.
S97   The swimmers.
T66   Tom sails away.
T97   Two little flowers.
W17   Walking.
W24   Walt Whitman.
W52   West London.
W62   The white gulls.
Performers: Ted Puffer, tenor; pianist not verified.
Folkways FM-3346/7. 4s. 12in. 33rpm. R64-1688.
S751   Violin sonata no. 1.
S752   Violin sonata no. 2.
S753   Violin sonata no. 3.
S754   Violin sonata no. 4.
Performers: Paul Zukofsky, violin; Gilbert Kalish, piano.
Folkways FM-3348. 2s. 12in. 33rpm. R64-1204.
The short piano pieces.
A63   Anti-abolitionist riots.
P96   Varied air with protests.
S71   Some southpaw pitching.
S741   In the inn.
T53   Three-page sonata.
T96   Twenty-two.
Performer: James Sykes, piano.
Folkways FM-3369. 2s. 12in. 33rpm. R67-3330.
Q2   String quartet no. 2.
Performers: Walden String Quartet.
With: Piano concerto no. 1, by A. Hovhaness.
Lehigh 1134. 2s. 12in. 33rpm.
S73   A son of a gambolier.
Performers: Lehigh University Concert Band.
Other contents not verified.
Louisville LOU-621. 2s. 12in. 33rpm. R62-257.
H75   Decoration day.
Performers: Louisville Orchestra; Robert Whitney, conductor.
With: Suite for symphonic strings, by L. Harrison.
Louisville LOU-651. 2s. 12in. 33rpm. R65-528.
V33   Variations on America.
Performers: Louisville Orchestra; Robert Whitney, conductor.

With: Umbrian suite, by U. Kay.—Concerto for wind quintet and
orchestra, by A. Etler.
Lyrichord LL-17. 2s. 12in. 33rpm.
  S751   Violin sonata no. 1.
  S753   Violin sonata no. 3.
  Performers: Joan Field, violin; Leopold Mittman, piano.
MGM Records MGM-E-3454. 2s. 12in. 33rpm. R57-222.
  S754   Violin sonata no. 4.
  Performers: Anahid Ajemian, violin; Maro Ajemian, piano.
Mercury MG-50096. 2s. 12in. 33rpm. RA57-97.
  S751   Violin sonata no. 1.
  S752   Violin sonata no. 2.
  Performers: Rafael Druian, violin; John Simms, piano.
Mercury MG-50097. 2s. 12in. 33rpm. RA57-98.
  S753   Violin sonata no. 3.
  S754   Violin sonata no. 4.
  Performers: Rafael Druian, violin; John Simms, piano.
Mercury MG-50149. 2s. 12in. 33rpm. R60-668.
  S993   Symphony no. 3.
  T54   Three places in New England.
  Performers: Eastman-Rochester Symphony Orchestra;
  Howard Hanson, conductor.
  x: Mercury SR-90149st.
Mercury MG-50442. 2s. 12in. 33rpm. RA67-117.
  S754   Violin sonata no. 4.
  Performers: Joseph Szigeti, violin; Roy Bogas, piano.
  With: Violin sonata, by C. Debussy.—Violin sonata no. 1,
  by A. Honneger.—Stücke, op. 7, by A. von Webern.
  x: Mercury SR-90442st.
Mercury SR-90149st. 2s. 12in. 33rpm.
  see: Mercury MG-50149.
Mercury SR-90442st. 2s. 12in. 33rpm.
  see: Mercury MG-50442.
Music Library MLR-7071. 2s. 12in. 33rpm.
  Contemporary choral music.
  H33   Harvest home.
  P976   Psalm 67.
  Performers: Columbia Teachers College Choir; Dorothy Ohl, organ;
  Harry R. Wilson, conductor.
  With: A thing of beauty, by H. R. Wilson.—To everything there is
  a season, by M. Rózsa.
New Music Quarterly Records NMQR-1013. [?]s. 12in. 78[?]rpm.
  Barn dance [title not verified].

H75   Washington's birthday.
S56   In the night.
Performers: Pan-American Orchestra; Nicolas Slominsky, conductor.
With: Lilacs and toys, by C. Ruggles.
x: New Music Quarterly Records NMQR-I-5.
New Music Quarterly Records NMQR-1112. [?]s. [?]in. 78[?]rpm.
G33   General William Booth's entrance into heaven.
Performers: Radiana Pazmor, soprano; Généviève Pittot, piano.
With: Airplane sonata, by G. Antheil.
x: New Music Quarterly Records NMQR-II-4.
New Music Quarterly Records NMQR-1412. 2s. 12in. 33rpm.
A61   Ann Street.
C47   Charlie Rutlage.
E93   Evening.
G78   The greatest man.
R43   Resolution.
T97   Two little flowers.
Performers: Mordecai Baumann, bass; Albert Hirsch, piano.
New Music Quarterly Records NMQR-1612. 2s. 12in. 33rpm.
S754   Violin sonata no. 4.
Performers: Joseph Szigeti, violin; Andor Foldes, piano.
New Music Quarterly Records NMQR-I-5.
see: New Music Quarterly Records NMQR-1013.
New Music Quarterly Records NMQR-II-4.
see: New Music Quarterly Records NMQR-1112.
New Records NRLP-305. 2s. 12in. 33rpm.
P976   Psalm 67.
Performers: Hamline University A Cappella Choir; Robert Holliday,
    conductor.
With works by Krenek and others.
Nonesuch 1169. 2s. 12in. 33rpm.
see: Nonesuch H-71169st.
Nonesuch H-71169st. 2s. 12in. 33rpm. R67-1635.
S741   Piano sonata no. 1.
Performer: Noël Lee.
x: Nonesuch 1169.
Nonesuch H-71200st. 2s. 12in. 33rpm. R68-1377.
Yankee organ music.
A23   Adeste fideles in an organ prelude.
V31   Variations on America.
Performer: Richard Ellsasser, organ.
With works by G. W. Chadwick, J. K. Paine, and C. Hewitt.
Nonesuch H-71209st. 2s. 12in. 33rpm. R68-1649.

A61   Ann Street.
A88   At the river.
C13   The cage.
C47   Charlie Rutlage.
C58   A Christmas carol.
E93   Evening.
F24   A farewell to land.
G33   General William Booth enters into heaven.
G78   The greatest man.
S62   Side show.
S69   Soliloquy.
S97   From The swimmers.
W52   West London.
Performers: Marni Nixon, soprano; John McCabe, piano.
With: Songs from the Japanese, by A. Goehr.—Chuench'i,
    by G. Schürmann.
Nonesuch H-71222st. 2s. 12in. 33rpm. 75-760576.
American brass music.
C59   Chrômatimelôdtune.
F93   From the steeples.
S769   Song for a harvest season.
Performers: American Brass Quintet; carillon of Riverside Church,
    New York; Jan De Gaetani, mezzo-soprano.
With: Quintet for brass, by A. Brehm.—The fourth millennium,
    by H. Brant.—Music for brass quintet, by P. Phillips.
Oceanic OCS-31. 2s. 10in. 33rpm.
S56   A set of pieces for orchestra and piano.
Performers: Stell Anderson, piano; Vienna State Opera Orchestra;
    Jonathan Sternberg, conductor.
With: Fantaisie pastorale, by D. Milhaud.
Odyssey 32-16-0059. 2s. 12in. 33rpm. R67-2825.
S741   Piano sonata no. 1.
Performer: William Masselos.
Odyssey 32-16-0161. 2s. 12in. 33rpm. R67-3726.
Music of our time.
Q1   Three quarter-tone pieces for two pianos.
Performers: George C. Papastavrou, Stuart Warren Lanning, pianos.
With: One-three quarters, by T. Macero.—Triple play, by C. Hampton.
    —Lines for the fallen, by D. Lybbert.—Catch-up, by C. Hampton.
x: Odyssey 32-16-0162st.
Odyssey 32-16-0162st. 2s. 12in. 33rpm. R67-3727.
see: Odyssey 32-16-0161.

Overtone LP-7. 2s. 12in. 33rpm. RA56-75.
A14   Abide with me.
A61   Ann Street.
A88   At the river.
A94   Autumn.
B48   Berceuse.
C54   The children's hour.
D61   Disclosure.
E93   Evening.
G33   General William Booth enters into heaven.
G78   The greatest man.
H29   Harpalus.
H44   He is there.
I38   In Flanders field.
M29   Maple leaves.
O61   One, two, three.
S47   The see'r.
S52   Serenity.
S769   Song for a harvest season.
S97   The swimmers.
T19   Tarrant moss.
T66   Tom sails away.
T97   Two little flowers.
W17   Walking.
W61   Where the eagle.
W62   The white gulls.
Performers: Helen Boatwright, soprano; John Kirkpatrick, piano.
Period SPLP-501. 2s. 12in. 33rpm.
Q2   String quartet no. 2.
Performers: Walden String Quartet.
Phillips 9018/9. 4s. 12in. 33rpm.
see: Phillips PHC-2-002st.
Phillips PHC-2-002st. 4s. 12in. 33rpm. R68-137.
S751   Violin sonata no. 1.
S752   Violin sonata no. 2.
S753   Violin sonata no. 3.
S754   Violin sonata no. 4.
Performers: Rafael Druian, violin; John Simms, piano.
With: Violin sonata no. 2, by B. Bartók.
x: Phillips 9018/9. x: Phillips WSM-2-002.
Phillips WSM-2-002. 4s. 12in. 33rpm. R68-137.
see: Phillips PHC-2-002st.

Polymusic PRLP-1001. 2s. 12in. 33rpm.
    The music of Charles Ives, vol. 1.
    C41   Central Park in the dark.
    C752   Violin sonata no. 2.
    H19   Hallowe'en.
    L31   Trio for piano, clarinet and violin.
    O96   Over the pavements.
    U54   The unanswered question.
    Performers: Polymusic Chamber Orchestra; Elliot Magaziner, violin;
        Frank Glazer, piano; David Weber, clarinet; Vladimir Cherniavsky,
        conductor.
Pye GGC-4104. 2s. 12in. 33rpm.
    Q11   Quartet no. 1.
    Performers: Amici Quartet.
Pye GGC-4105.
    [Contains 13 songs; contents not verified.]
    Performers: Marni Nixon, soprano; John McCabe, piano.
RCA Victor LM-2676. 2s. 12in. 33rpm.
    The Robert Shaw Chorale on tour.
    H33   Harvest home chorales.
    Performers: Robert Shaw Chorale and orchestra; Robert Shaw,
        conductor.
    With: Trois chansons, by M. Ravel.—The nightingale.—
    Sometimes I feel like a moanin' dove.—Vesperae solemnes de
    confessore, K.339, by W. A. Mozart.—Friede auf Erden, by
    A. Schönberg.
    x: RCA Victor LSC-2676st.
RCA Victor LM-2893. 2s. 12in. 33rpm. R66-846, R66-847.
    S991   Symphony no. 1.
    U54   The answered question.
    V33   Variations on America.
    Performers: Chicago Symphony Orchestra; Morton Gould, conductor.
    x: RCA Victor LSC-2893st.
RCA Victor LM-2941. 2s. 12in. 33rpm. R67-2583.
    S741   Piano sonata no. 1.
    Performer: William Masselos.
    x: RCA Victor LSC-2941st.
RCA Victor LM-2959. 2s. 12in. 33rpm. R67-3108.
    O65   Orchestral set no. 2.
    R64   Browning overture.
    T54   Putnam's camp.
    Performers: Chicago Symphony Orchestra; Morton Gould, conductor.

RCA Victor LSC-2676st. 2s. 12in. 33rpm.
see: RCA Victor LM-2676.
RCA Victor LSC-2893st. 2s. 12in. 33rpm. R66-948, R66-949.
see: RCA Victor LM-2893.
RCA Victor LSC-2941st. 2s. 12in. 33rpm. R67-2584.
see: RCA Victor LM-2941.
RCA Victor LSC-2959st. 2s. 12in. 33rpm. R67-3109.
see: RCA Victor LM-2959.
Recorded Publications Co. CC-3. 2s. 12in. 33rpm.
Choral music of the 20th century.
P976   Psalm 67.
Performers: Illinois Wesleyan University Choir; Lewis E. Whikehart,
conductor.
With works by A. Schönberg, E. Toch, L. Whikehart, R. Thompson,
A Ginastera, N. Lockwood, G. Oldroyd, F. Poulenc.
Sheffield 3. 2s. 12in. 33rpm.
L31   Largo for piano, clarinet and violin.
Performers: Compinsky Ensemble; Maurice Compinsky, violin;
Kalmar Bloch, clarinet; Sara Compinsky, piano.
With: Quartet in Eb, op. 16, by L. van Beethoven.—Trio for piano
and strings, op. 1, by C. Franck.—Suite for violin, clarinet
and piano, by D. Milhaud.—Poems to Martha, by E. Toch.
x: Sheffield S-3st.
Sheffield S-3st. 2s. 12in. 33rpm.
see: Sheffield 3.
Siena S-100-2. 2s. 12in. 33rpm. R61-872.
U54   The unanswered question.
Performers: Zimbler Sinfonietta; Roger Voisin, trumpet; Lukas Foss,
conductor.
With: Symphonies pour petite orchestra, no. 4, by D. Milhaud.—
Little suite, by N. Skalkattos.—Divertimento, by B. Bartók.
Society for the Preservation of the American Musical Heritage MTA-116.
2s. 12in. 33rpm.
Choral music of the 20th century.
C58   A Christmas carol.
P976   Psalm 67.
T95   Turn ye, turn ye.
Performers: Helen Heir, soprano; John Jaeger, baritone; Hamline
University A Cappella Choir; Robert Holliday, conductor.
With works by Russell Harris, E. Carter, R. Raffman, G. Glasow,
P. Fetler, K. Gaburo, G. Antheil.

204

Society of Participating Artists SPA-9. 2s. 12in. 33rpm.
  A86   At parting.
  A87   At sea.
  A88   At the river.
  C58   A Christmas carol.
  I17   I'll not complain.
  I42   In summer fields.
  M69 Mists.
  N71   A night thought.
  T65   Tolerance.
  W24 Walt Whitman.
  W57 When the stars are in quiet skies.
  Performers: Jacqueline Greissle, soprano; Joseph Wolman, piano.
  With songs by S. Revueltas.
Society of Participating Artists SPA-39. 2s. 12in. 33rpm. R54-450.
  S992 Symphony no. 2.
  Performers: Vienna Philharmonic; Frederick Adler, conductor.
Time 58005. 2s. 12in. 33rpm. RA63-54.
  S742 Piano sonata no. 2.
  Performers: Aloys Kontarsky, piano; Theo Plümacher, viola;
    Willy Schwegler, flute.
  x: Time S-8005st.
Time S-8005. 2s. 12in. 33rpm. R63-1673.
  see: Time 58005.
Turnabout TV-34146Sst. 2s. 12in. 33rpm. R68-910.
  H75   Holidays.
  Performers: Southern Methodist University Choir; Dallas Symphony
    Orchestra; Donald Johanos, conductor.
  With: Vocalise, by S. Rachmaminoff.—Symphonic dances,
    by S. Rachmaninoff.
Turnabout TV-34154st. 2s. 12in. 33rpm.
  U54   The unanswered question.
  Performers: Roger Voisin, trumpet; Zimbler Sinfonietta;
    Lukas Foss, conductor.
  With: Symphonies pour petite orchestra, no. 4, by D. Milhaud.—
    Little suite, by N. Skalkottas.—Divertimento, by Bartók.
Turnabout TV-34157st. 2s. 12in. 33rpm.
  Q11   String quartet no. 1.
  Q2   String quartet no. 2.
  Performers: Kohon Quartet.
Unicorn UNLP-1037. 2s. 12in. 33rpm. RA57-48.
  U54   The unanswered question.

Performers: Zimbler Sinfonietta; Roger Voisin, trumpet;
Lukas Foss, conductor.
Vanguard C-10032/4. 6s. 12in. 33rpm.
H19   Hallowe'en.
S991   Symphony no. 1.
S992   Symphony no. 2.
S993   Symphony no. 3.
S994   Symphony no. 4.
Performers: New Philharmonia of London; Ambrosian Singers;
Harold Farberman, conductor.
x: Vanguard VCS-10032/4st.
Vanguard VCS-10013st. 2s. 12in. 33rpm. R67-1815.
C67   The circus band march.
R64   Robert Browning overture.
S56   Set for theatre orchestra.
U54   The unanswered question.
Performers: New Philharmonia of London; Harold Farberman,
conductor.
Vanguard VCS-10032/4st. 6s. 12in. 33rpm. R68-601.
see: Vanguard C-10032/4.
Vanguard VRS-468. 2s. 12in. 33rpm. R55-653.
S993   Symphony no. 3.
Performers: Baltimore Little Symphony; Reginald Stewart, conductor.
With: Suite for oboe & string orchestra, by R. Donovan.
Vox DL-1120. 2s. 12in. 33rpm.
Q11   String quartet no. 1.
Q2   String quartet no. 2.
Performers: Kohon String Quartet.
x: Vox STDL-501.120st.
Vox STDL-501120st. 2s. 12in. 33rpm. R64-311.
see: Vox DL-1120.
WCFM LP-1. 2s. 12in. 33rpm. R61-1892.
S993   Symphony no. 3.
Performers: National Gallery of Art Orchestra; Richard Bales,
conductor.
With: Music of the American Revolution, suite no. 1, by R. Bales.
Yaddo I-2.
H98   Hymn.
L37   The last reader.
Performers and additional contents not verified.

Performer Index

Adler, Frederick Charles, 1889–1959
[conductor]:
    Society of Participating Artists
    SPA-39.
Ajemian, Anahid [violinist]:
    MGM Records MGM-E-3454.
Ajemian, Maro [pianist]:
    MGM Records MGM-E-3454.
Ambrosian Singers:
    Vanguard C-10032/4.
    Vanguard VCS-10032/4st.
American Brass Quintet:
    Nonesuch H-71222st.
American Recording Society
Orchestra:
    American Recording Society
    ARS-27.
    American Recording Society
    ARS-116.
American Symphony Orchestra:
    Columbia D3S-783.
    Columbia ML-6175.

    Columbia ML-6415.
    Columbia MS-7015st.
    Columbia MS-6775st.
Amici String Quartet:
    Pye GGC-4104.
Anderson, Stell [pianist]:
    Oceanic OCS-31.
Babitz, Sol [violinist]:
    Alco 101/2.
Bales, Richard Horner, 1915–
[conductor]:
    WCFM LP-1.
Baltimore Little Symphony:
    Vanguard VRS-468.
Baumann, Mordecai [bass]:
    New Music Quarterly Records
    NMQR-1412.
Bernstein, Leonard, 1918–
[conductor]:
    Columbia D3S-783.
    Columbia KL-5489.
    Columbia KS-6155st.

Columbia ML-6243.
Columbia ML-6289.
Columbia ML-6415.
Columbia MS-6843st.
Columbia MS-6889st.
Columbia MS-7015st.
Columbia MS-7147st.
Biggs, Edward George Power, 1906–
[organist]:
Columbia ML-5496.
Columbia MS-6161st.
Bloch, Kalman [clarinettist]:
Sheffield 3.
Sheffield S-3st.
Boatwright, Helen (Strassburger)
[soprano]:
Overtone LP-7.
x: Strassburger, Helen.
Bogas, Roy [pianist]:
Mercury MG-50442.
Mercury SR-90442st.
Boston Chamber Ensemble:
Cambridge 804.
Cambridge CRS-1804st.
Camerata Singers:
Columbia MS-7147.
Cherniavsky, Vladimir [conductor]:
Polymusic PRLP-1001.
Chicago Symphony Orchestra:
RCA Victor LM-2893.
RCA Victor LM-2959.
RCA Victor LSC-2893st.
RCA Victor LSC-2959st.
Columbia Chamber Orchestra:
Columbia ML-6321.
Columbia MS-6921st.
Columbia University. Teachers
College. Choir:
Music Library MLR-7071.
Compinsky, Maurice [violinist]:
Sheffield 3.
Sheffield S-3st.
Compinsky, Sara [pianist]:

Sheffield 3.
Sheffield S-3st.
Compinsky Ensemble:
Sheffield 3.
Sheffield S-3st.
Crossman, Joann [pianist]:
Educo 4006.
Curry, Corrine [mezzo-soprano]:
Cambridge 804.
Cambridge CRS-1804st.
Dahl, Ingolf, 1912–   [pianist]:
Alco 101/2.
Dallas Symphony Orchestra:
Turnabout TV-34146Sst.
De Gaetani, Jan [mezzo-soprano]:
Nonesuch H-71222st.
Druian, Rafael [violinist]:
Mercury MG-50096.
Mercury MG-50097.
Phillips PHC-2-002st.
Phillips WSM-2-002.
Eastman-Rochester Symphony
Orchestra:
Mercury MG-50149.
Mercury SR-90149st.
Ellsasser, Richard [organist]:
Nonesuch H-71200st.
Engel, Lehman, 1910-
[conductor]:
Columbia 17139D.
Farberman, Harold, 1929–
[conductor]:
Cambridge 804.
Cambridge CRS-1804st.
Vanguard C-10032/4.
Vanguard VCS-10013st.
Vanguard VCS-10032/4st.
Field, Joan [violinist]:
Lyrichord LL-17.
Filharmoniske Selskap, Oslo.
Orkester:
Composers Recordings, Inc.
CRI-163.

x: Oslo Philharmonic
Orchestra.
Finnish National Radio Symphony
Orchestra:
Composers Recordings, Inc.
CRI-190SD.
Foldes, Andor, 1913–   [pianist]:
New Music Quarterly Records
NMQR-1612.
Foss, Lukas, 1922–   [conductor]:
Turnabout TV-34154st.
Siena S-100-2.
Unicorn UNLP-1037.
Friedberg, Ruth [pianist]:
Duke.
Glazer, Frank [pianist]:
Polymusic PRLP-1001.
Göteborg Symphony Orchestra:
see:
Göteborgs Symfoniorchester.
Göteborg Symfoniorchester:
Composers Recordings, Inc.
CRI-180.
Composers Recordings, Inc.
CRI-190SDst.
x Göteborg Symphony
Orchestra.
Gould, Morton, 1913–
[conductor]:
RCA Victor LM-2893.
RCA Victor LM-2959.
RCA Victor LSC-2893st.
RCA Victor LSC-2959st.
Gramm, Donald [singer]:
Desto D411/2.
Gregg Smith Singers:
Columbia ML-6321.
Columbia MS-6921st.
Greissle, Jacqueline [soprano]:
Society of Participating Artists
SPA-9.

Hamline University, St. Paul.
A Cappella Choir:
New Records NRLP-305.
Society for the Preservation
of the American Musical
Heritage MTA-116.
Hanks, John Kennedy [tenor]:
Duke.
Hanson, Howard, 1896–
[conductor]:
Mercury MG-50149.
Mercury SR-90149st.
Heir, Helen [soprano]:
Society for the Preservation
of the American Musical
Heritage MTA-116.
Hendl, Walter, 1917–
[conductor]:
American Recording Society
ARS-27.
American Recording Society
ARS-116.
Desto 403.
Desto DST-6403st.
Herz, Otto, 1894–   [pianist]:
Columbia ML-2169.
Columbia MM-987.
Concert Hall CH C-7.
Hirsch, Albert [pianist]:
New Music Quarterly Records
NMQR-1412.
Holliday, Robert [conductor]:
New Records NRLP-305.
Society for the Preservation of
the American Musical
Heritage MTA-116.
Iceland State Radio Chorus:
Composers Recordings, Inc.
CRI-177.
Composers Recordings, Inc.
CRI-190SDst.

Iceland Symphony Orchestra:
Composers Recordings, Inc.
CRI-177.
Composers Recordings, Inc.
CRI-190SDst.
Illinois Wesleyan University.
Collegiate Choir:
Recorded Publications Co.
CC-3.
Imperial Philharmonic Symphony
Orchestra, Tokyo:
Composers Recordings, Inc.
CRI-163.
Composers Recordings, Inc.
CRI-190SDst.
x: Tokyo Imperial
Philharmonic Orchestra.
Ithaca College, Ithaca, N. Y.
Concert Choir:
Columbia ML-5321.
Columbia MS-6921st.
Jaeger, John [baritone]:
Society for the Preservation of
the American Musical
Heritage MTA-116.
Janssen, Werner, 1899–
[conductor]:
Artist 1404.
Artist JS-13.
Artist LP-100.
Everest 3118st.
Everest 6118.
Janssen Symphony Orchestra.
Artist 1404.
Artist JS-13.
Artist LP-100.
Everest 3118st.
Everest 6118.
x: Los Angeles Orchestra.
Johanos, Donald, 1928–
[conductor]:
Turnabout TV-34146Sst.

Juilliard String Quartet.
CBS 72630.
Columbia ML-6427.
Columbia MS-7027st.
Kalish, Gilbert [pianist]:
Folkways FM-3346/7.
Katz, David [conductor]:
Columbia ML-6175.
Columbia MS-6775st.
Kirkpatrick, John, 1905–
[pianist]:
Columbia 72535/9D.
Columbia ML-4250.
Columbia MM-749.
Columbia MS-7192st.
Overtone LP-7.
Kohon String Quartet.
Turnabout TV-34157st.
Vox DL-1120.
Vox STDL-501.120st.
Kontarsky, Aloys, 1931–
[pianist]:
Time 58005.
Time S-8005st.
Lanning, Stuart Warren [pianist]:
Odyssey 32-16-0161.
Odyssey 32-16-0162st.
Lee, Noël, 1924–   [pianist]:
Nonesuch 1169.
Nonesuch H-71169st.
Lehigh University. Concert Band.
Lehigh 1134.
Lichter, Bonnie [flutist]:
Composers Recordings, Inc.
CRI-150.
Lipkin, Seymour [conductor]:
Columbia ML-6289.
Columbia MS-6889st.
Los Angeles Orchestra:
see: Janssen Symphony
Orchestra.
Louisville Orchestra:

Louisville LOU-621.
Louisville LOU-651.
McCabe, John, 1939–   [pianist]:
  Pye GGC-4105.
McChesney, Ernest [tenor]:
  Concert Hall CH C-7.
Madrigal Singers.
  Columbia 17139D.
Magazinger, Elliot [violinist]:
  Polymusic PRLP-1001.
Mandel, Alan [pianist]:
  Desto 6458/61.
Masselos, William [pianist]:
  Columbia ML-4490.
  Odyssey 32-16-0059.
  RCA Victor LM-2941.
  RCA Victor LSC-2941st.
Mittman, Leopold, 1904–
  [pianist]:
  Lyrichord LL-17.
National Gallery of Art Orchestra:
  see: U. S. National Gallery of
  Art. Orchestra.
New Philharmonia Orchestra,
  London:
  Vanguard C-10032/4.
  Vanguard VCS-10032/4st.
New York Philharmonic Orchestra:
  see: Philharmonic Symphony-
  Society of New York.
Nieuw Amsterdam Trio.
  Decca DG-710.126st.
  Decca DL-10126.
Nixon, Marni [soprano]:
  Pye GGC-4105.
Ohl, Dorothy [organist]:
  Music Library MLR-7071.
Ormandy, Eugene, 1899–
  [conductor]:
  Columbia D3S-783.
  Columbia ML-6084.
  Columbia ML-6415.
  Columbia MS-6684st.

Columbia MS-7015st.
Columbia MS-7111st.
Oslo Philharmonic Orchestra:
  see: Filharmoniske Selskap,
  Oslo. Orkester.
Ozawa, Seiji, 1935–
  [conductor]:
  Columbia ML-6243.
  Columbia MS-6843st.
Pan-American Orchestra.
  New Music Quarterly Records
  NMQR-I-5.
  New Music Quarterly Records
  NMQR-1013.
Papa-stavrou, George [pianist]:
  Composers Recordings, Inc.
  CRI-150.
  Odyssey 32-16-0161.
  Odyssey 32-16-0162st.
Pazmor, Radian [soprano]:
  New Music Quarterly Records
  NMQR-II-4.
  New Music Quarterly Records
  NMQR-1112.
Peress, Maurice [pianist]:
  Columbia ML-6243.
  Columbia MS-6843st.
Philadelphia Orchestra:
  Columbia D3S-783.
  Columbia ML-6084.
  Columbia ML-6415.
  Columbia MS-6684st.
  Columbia MS-7015st.
  Columbia MS-7111st.
Philharmonic-Symphony Society
  of New York:
  Columbia D3S-783.
  Columbia KL-5489.
  Columbia KS-6155st.
  Columbia ML-6243.
  Columbia ML-6289.
  Columbia ML-6415.
  Columbia MS-6843st.

211

Columbia MS-6889st.
Columbia MS-7015st.
Columbia MS-7147st.
x: New York Philharmonic
  Orchestra.
Pittot, Geneviève [pianist]:
  New Music Quarterly Records
  NMQR-II-4.
  New Music Quarterly Records
  NMQR-1112.
Plümacher, Theo [violist]:
  Time 58005.
  Time S-8005st.
Polish National Radio Orchestra:
  see: Polskie Radio. Rozgłosnia
  Centralna, Warsaw.
  Orkiestra.
Polskie Radio. Rozgłosnia
  Centralna, Warsaw. Orkiestra.
  Composers Recordings, Inc.
  CRI-196SD.
Polymusic Chamber Orchestra:
  Polymusic PRLP-1001.
Puffer, Ted [tenor]:
  Folkways 3344/5.
Robert Shaw Chorale.
  RCA Victor LM-2676.
  RCA Victor LSC-2676st.
Ross, Hugh, 1898–
  [conductor]:
  Columbia ML-6175.
  Columbia MS-6775st.
Royal Philharmonic Orchestra:
  Vanguard VCS-10013st.
Schola Cantorum, New York:
  Columbia D3S-783.
  Columbia ML-6175.
  Columbia MS-6775st.
Schwegler, Willy [flutist]:
  Time 58005.
  Time S-8005st.
Serebrier, José, 1938–
  [conductor]:

Columbia ML-6175.
Columbia MS-6775st.
Shaw, Robert Lawson, 1916–
  [conductor]:
  RCA Victor LM-2676.
  RCA Victor LSC-2676st.
Simms, John, pianist:
  Mercury ML-50096.
  Mercury MG-50097.
  Phillips PHC-2-002st.
  Phillips WSM-2-002.
Slonimsky, Nicolas, 1894–
  [conductor]:
  New Music Quarterly Records
  NMQR-1013.
  New Music Quarterly Records
  NMQR-I-5.
Southern Methodist University.
  Choir:
  Turnabout TV-34146Sst.
Stenberg, Jonathan [conductor]:
  Oceanic OCS-31.
Stewart, Reginald [conductor]:
  Vanguard VRS-468.
Stokowski, Leopold, 1882–
  [conductor]:
  Columbia D3S-783.
  Columbia ML-6175.
  Columbia ML-6415.
  Columbia MS-6775st.
  Columbia MS-7015st.
Strassburger, Helen:
  see: Boatwright, Helen
  (Strassburger).
Strickland, William [conductor]:
  Composers Recordings, Inc.
  CRI-163.
  Composers Recordings, Inc.
  CRI-177.
  Composers Recordings, Inc.
  CRI-180.
  Composers Recordings, Inc.
  CRI-190SD.

Composers Recordings, Inc.
CRI-196SD.
Sykes, James, 1908– [pianist]:
Folkways FM-3348.
Symonette, Randolph [bass]:
Columbia CLPS-1008.
Szigeti, Joseph, 1892–
[violinist]:
Mercury MG-50442.
Mercury SR-90442st.
New Music Quarterly Records
NMQR-1612.
Texas Boys' Choir:
Columbia ML-6321.
Columbia MS-6921st.
Tokyo Imperial Philharmonic
Orchestra:
see: Imperial Philharmonic
Symphony Orchestra, Tokyo.
Travers, Patricia, 1927–
[violinist]:
Columbia ML-2169.
Columbia MM-987.
U. S. National Gallery of Art.
Orchestra:
WCFM LP-1.
x: National Gallery of Art
Orchestra.
Vienna. Operntheater. Orchester:
Oceanic OCS-31.
x: Vienna State Opera
Orchestra.
Vienna Philharmonic Orchestra:
see: Wiener Philharmoniker.
Vienna State Opera Orchestra:
see: Vienna. Operntheater.
Orchester.
Vienna Symphony:
see: Wiener Symphoniker.
Voisin, Roger L., 1918–
[trumpeter]:

Siena S-100-2.
Turnabout TV-34154st.
Vosgerchian, Luise [pianist]:
Cambridge 804.
Cambridge CRS-1804st.
Walden String Quartet:
Disc 775.
Period SPLP-501.
Folkways FM-3369.
Weber, David [clarinettist]:
Polymusic PRLP-1001.
Whitney, Robert Sutton, 1904–
[conductor]:
Louisville LOU-621.
Louisville LOU-651.
Whikehart, Lewis E. [conductor]:
Recorded Publications Co.
CC-3.
Wiener Philharmoniker:
Society of Participating Artists
SPA-39.
x: Vienna Philharmonic
Orchestra.
Wiener Symphoniker:
Desto 403.
Desto DST-6403st.
Society of Participating Artists
SPA-39.
x: Vienna Symphony.
Wilson, Harry Robert, 1901–
[conductor]:
Music Library MLR-7071.
Wolman, Joseph [pianist]:
Society of Participating Artists
SPA-9.
Zimbler Sinfonietta:
Siena S-100-2.
Turnabout TV-34154st.
Unicorn UNLP-1037.
Zukofsky, Paul, 1943–
[violinist]:
Folkways FM-3346/7.

LIBRARY
OKALOOSA - WALTON JUNIOR COLLEGE

OKALOOSA WALTON JUNIOR COLLEGE

1000005528